HOW TO BUILD CLASSIC
Garden Furniture

Danny Proulx

POPULAR WOODWORKING BOOKS
CINCINNATI, OHIO

How to Build Classic Garden Furniture. Copyright © 1999 by Danny Proulx. Manufactured in the United States of America. All rights reserved. No part of this book may be reproduced in any form or by any electronic or mechanical means including information storage and retrieval systems without permission in writing from the publisher, except by a reviewer, who may quote brief passages in a review. Published by Popular Woodworking Books, an imprint of F&W Publications, Inc., 1507 Dana Avenue, Cincinnati, Ohio 45207. (800) 289-0963. First edition.

Other fine Popular Woodworking Books are available from your local bookstore, woodworking store or direct from the publisher.

03   02   01   00   99   5   4   3   2   1

Library of Congress Cataloging-in-Publication Data

Proulx, Danny
    How to build classic garden furniture / Danny Proulx.—1st ed.
        p.   cm.
    Includes index.
    ISBN 1-55870-483-3 (pbk. : alk. paper)
    1. Outdoor furniture—Design and construction. 2. Garden ornaments and furniture—Design and construction. 3. Furniture making. I. Title.
TT197.5.O9P76   1999
684.1′8—dc21   98-39468
                                                         CIP

Editor: Bruce E. Stoker
Production editor: Nicole R. Klungle
Interior designer: Sandy Conopeotis Kent
Cover designer: Angela Lennert Wilcox
Production coordinator: Erin Boggs

Credits
Step-by-Step Photography: Danny Proulx
Computer illustrations: Bruce E. Stoker and Joseph Bradley ("Dining Table," page 17; "Dining Chair," page 18; "Garden Bench," page 29; "Octagon Table," page 37; "Garden Wishing Well," page 55; "Shingle Layout," page 59)
Cover and Completed Project Photography: Michael Bowie, Lux Photographic, 95A Beech St., Suite 204, Ottawa, Ontario K1S 3J7
Garden Location: Trudie Lentz, Russell, Ontario
Workshop: Rideau Cabinets, P.O. Box 331, Russell, Ontario K4R 1E1

READ THIS IMPORTANT SAFETY NOTICE To prevent accidents, keep safety in mind while you work. Use the safety guards installed on power equipment; they are for your protection. When working on power equipment, keep fingers away from saw blades, wear safety goggles to prevent injuries from flying wood chips and sawdust, wear headphones to protect your hearing, and consider installing a dust vacuum to reduce the amount of airborne sawdust in your woodshop. Don't wear loose clothing, such as neckties or shirts with loose sleeves, or jewelry, such as rings, necklaces or bracelets, when working on power equipment, and tie back long hair to prevent it from getting caught in your equipment. The author and editors who compiled this book have tried to make the contents as accurate and correct as possible. Plans, illustrations, photographs and text have been carefully checked. All instructions, plans and projects should be carefully read, studied and understood before beginning construction. Due to the variability of local conditions, construction materials, skill levels, etc., neither the author nor Popular Woodworking Books assumes any responsibility for any accidents, injuries, damages or other losses incurred resulting from the material presented in this book.

METRIC CONVERSION CHART		
TO CONVERT	**TO**	**MULTIPLY BY**
Inches	Centimeters	2.54
Centimeters	Inches	0.4
Feet	Centimeters	30.5
Centimeters	Feet	0.03
Yards	Meters	0.9
Meters	Yards	1.1
Sq. Inches	Sq. Centimeters	6.45
Sq. Centimeters	Sq. Inches	0.16
Sq. Feet	Sq. Meters	0.09
Sq. Meters	Sq. Feet	10.8
Sq. Yards	Sq. Meters	0.8
Sq. Meters	Sq. Yards	1.2
Pounds	Kilograms	0.45
Kilograms	Pounds	2.2
Ounces	Grams	28.4
Grams	Ounces	0.04

ACKNOWLEDGMENTS

As always, there are dozens of people who make writing these books more pleasure than work. To my wife, Gale, who is always supportive. And, to my father-in-law, Jack Chaters, who was my model and assistant, I can't thank you enough for helping me build these projects.

Adam Blake, Bruce Stoker and all the crew at Popular Woodworking Books are always there with help and advice, and are ready to tackle anything I need done. Without their support, this book would not have happened. They're quite an impressive team!

The completed project photographs were done in a garden lovingly created by Trudie Lentz of Russell, Ontario. It is an astounding setting that enhanced the projects.

And to Michael Bowie and his assistant, Katya Doleatto—along with all the others whom I've forgotten to mention—they're always around and ready to help when I need them.

ABOUT THE AUTHOR

Danny Proulx, a resident of Russell, Ontario, has been involved in woodworking for more than 30 years and has run his own kitchen and bathroom remodeling shop since 1989. He has helped countless woodworkers, both hobbyists and professionals, improve their skills through many workshops and seminars. He has written *Build Your Own Kitchen Cabinets*, *Do-It-Yourself Kitchen Cabinetmaking* and *The Kitchen Cabinetmaker's Building and Business Manual*, as well as many articles for *Cabinetmaker Magazine*, *Canadian Workshop*, *Popular Woodworking* and *Woodshop News*. He also publishes a free Internet newsletter providing information for hobbyists and professional woodworkers. To subscribe, write the author at danny@cabinetmaking.com.

HOW TO USE THIS BOOK

Some of us are intimidated by complex-looking woodworking projects. And a few of the designs in this book, when viewed in their entirety, look complicated. However, don't be overwhelmed by the total project. Break the sections into small workable units. Analyze each joint and how it interacts with the project as a whole. For example, a chair has two back and front leg assemblies with parts fitted to form the back and seat. There are a couple of stringers for support, and two arms. Nothing complicated—just a few pieces of wood joined together in well defined ways.

There's a great deal of satisfaction in building these projects. And best of all, a great deal of enjoyment in using them for years to come. The structures and furniture are built to last. All that's required is a little care and maintenance.

Table *of* Contents

page 16

page 28

page 36

page 44

page 54

page 64

page 70

page 88

page 98

page 80

page 108

CHAPTER 1

Before You Get Started

Classic Garden Bench (page 28)

Summertime and enjoying the outdoors on our patios and decks brings a flood of warm memories to many of us. People who live in the warmer southern climates get to spend a great deal of time living outdoors, while those of us in the northern climates have but a few precious months to cram in all the outdoor activities we've been dreaming about during the long, cold winter. But no matter if it's for two or twelve months, most people want luscious gardens and beautiful decks with comfortable furniture.

I am a cabinetmaker, specializing in kitchen cabinets. However, I love nothing better than sitting on a comfortable chair in my backyard during those warm summer months. Unfortunately, kitchen cabinetmaking and the great outdoors aren't normally associated with each other. I'm either in the shop or installing a kitchen and dreaming

Seated Arbor (page 103)

of being outside. So far, I haven't had anyone ask me to install a kitchen in their garden.

To get around my summer indoor problem, I've added deck and outdoor furniture building to my list of business services. It's a little selfish because, as much as I enjoy building decks, the real motive is to be out in the summer sun. Luckily, most of my clients are thinking more about decks, patios and gardens in the summer and less about kitchens. We all end up winners: I get to work outside and they get the deck they've been planning for years.

As soon as the deck or patio has been completed, most of us turn our attention to outdoor furniture. Those who are avid gardeners start looking for the little extras that will turn their garden into a peaceful retreat. Woodworkers who are outdoor living enthusiasts have an advantage—the opportunity to create some wonderful and useful pieces of furniture or garden accessories for those spaces, and save quite a bit of money in the process.

Outdoor Considerations

There are, of course, some special techniques and applications that must be taken into account when building outdoor furniture. We are subjecting wood and metal to some aggressive climatic conditions that don't often re-spect your handiwork. Rain, wind, sun and cold temperatures can dramatically shorten the useful life of any piece of unprotected wooden furniture. However, with a little care and attention, we can prolong their useful lives.

In this book, we'll be dealing with wood types and their applications. Some species are better-suited for outdoor furniture and can be enjoyed almost indefinitely, with a few precautions. To illustrate that point, take a look at some of the antique wooden boats that are still traveling the waterways fifty years after they were created.

Hardware manufacturers have realized there is a growing demand for outdoor building materials and have introduced products that are suited for these specialized applications. Coated screws, galvanized bolts and other outdoor hardware will be detailed in this book.

And finally, one of the most important considerations is protecting your work with the right finish. These coatings are the primary guards against the elements, the first line of defense against one of wood's natural enemies—the weather. It's necessary to understand the properties of wood and its specific use in combination with the piece of furniture or structure we're building. We'll look at many of the protective coatings that are available.

The Projects

Building elegant, useful, long-lasting outdoor furniture and structures is well within the capabilities of all woodworkers. Some of the projects are challenging and others are relatively easy to build. The main goal, however, is to create a piece that will last for years. And when you consider the cost of purchasing good quality outdoor furniture and the hundreds of dollars saved by building them yourself, it's apparent the time and money have been well spent.

The first project is a beautiful outdoor dining set. It is a fine piece of furniture that will complement anyone's deck or patio. Why not enjoy the same elegance when dining outdoors as we do inside? There's no reason why we can't. You'll experience fine dining in the great outdoors with family and friends after building this high-class set.

After our fine dining experience, many of us look for a comfortable spot to sip a glass of wine and enjoy a good book. What could be nicer on a lazy summer evening? The garden bench will provide you with many years of comfort and, for some, become a favorite outdoor retreat. I'll illustrate a few style variations so you can build your perfect bench.

When we're entertaining, nothing is more useful than an elegant table filled with snacks and drinks. Most of the time we end up running around trying to "throw something together" to hold the punch bowl. Often it's an old table or a couple of boxes hastily covered with a cloth so our guests won't see the "handiwork." However, after completing the octagon patio table project, you'll never put on another table cover. This is a beautifully crafted piece of furniture that everyone will want to inspect.

I'll show the flower enthusiasts how to build a potpourri of planters. These are simple to construct and useful to own. Planters can be used on the deck, patio, around the yard or in front of the house to beautify and enhance the landscape. You also have the advantage of being able to move these planters around when you decide it's time for a change. That's a lot easier than transplanting a complete flower bed.

If you live in the country like I do, there's usually a wellhead pipe sticking out of the ground. I can't count the number of times someone has tripped on that darn pipe. The wishing well I built for this book will be covering my old "yard tripper." Whether or not you have a wellhead pipe or the perfect place in your garden for this lovely project doesn't matter. It's a great addition to any yard that will draw many positive comments from friends and neighbors.

Do you remember the barbecue balancing act at one of your backyard parties? That's when you were elected master barbecue chef and had to manage twenty hamburger patties and hot dogs, with buns and sauces, on the little side table of the barbecue. How about building a serving cart that acts as a side table during the cooking and a delivery cart when everyone is ready to eat? Complete the cooking, load up the cart and head on over to the table with the food. It's a simple and useful project that you'll use often. The serving cart also doubles as a portable snack table for those large garden parties.

Once all of the guests have gone and you long for a quiet, comfortable place to sit, how about relaxing on a garden swing? Nothing beats the peaceful relaxation of rocking back and forth on a swing. And you won't need to find a good tree limb to suspend the bench—it's all self-contained. The swing set is also strong and built to last. Strength is an important issue with any garden swing because you can be sure the little ones will try and launch the swing into the sky. There's always some brave little soul who tries to see how high the chair will go. It's also designed to come apart so it can be easily moved or stored for the winter months.

A trellis anchored in the ground or attached to the side of your house gives support to many types of flowering vines. They are simple to make and add a touch of class to any garden. Unlike the common wire trellis, these beautiful wooden variations look great long after the flowers have left the vines.

Probably one of the most comfortable pieces of outdoor furniture is the Adirondack-style chair or settee. To complete the ensemble, I've added an Adirondack coffee table. It's unusual to have a coffee table in the same design, so this full set will be a hit on any deck or patio.

An arbor tucked away in a secluded part of your flower garden will let you grow some of the beautiful varieties of climbing vines. But more importantly, the arbor's sheltered seat provides a resting place for the weary gardener, your private little oasis in the center of all your hard work. What better place to spend an hour or two sipping on a cool glass of lemonade? I'll also detail the construction of a barrel-ceiling walk-through arbor. This piece is an ideal passageway into your garden or yard, and it will look great once the flowering vine has taken hold.

And finally, the classic gazebo. Sitting and relaxing, by yourself or with friends, protected from the glaring sun or summer rain. Your private sheltered island in the backyard allows you to survey the results of all your hard work. What more could you ask for when all the world is rushing past? You'll get a great deal of satisfaction and spend many relaxing hours inside this structure.

CHAPTER 2

Outdoor Furniture Construction Techniques

Plan Your Project Needs

There are special precautions to be taken when building outdoor wood furniture. Unprotected wood, when exposed to the rain, wind and sun, will rot in a fairly short time. Some woods are more resistant to outdoor conditions than others, but for the most part, they should all be protected in certain ways so that their maximum useful life is achieved.

The type of wood, hardware used to connect the pieces and protective coatings applied are all important issues to consider.

Choosing a Wood Type

The first decision to make when building outdoor furniture is which type of wood to use. Softwoods such as redwood and cedar, as well as some hardwoods including mahogany, white oak and teak, have long been considered good "outdoor woods." The three hardwoods have been used in the boat-building industry for years.

The cost of these woods will also impact your decision, but it shouldn't be the most important issue. An inexpensive wood that will quickly rot outdoors is not cost-effective. Normally, cedar is the least expensive of the outdoor woods and teak is the most expensive. A wood option to consider is the family of pressure-treated woods. There are some special precautions to consider when working with this chemically treated wood; however, its relatively low price is attractive.

In general, softwoods from conifer trees grow faster and are therefore less expensive than hardwoods. Deciduous trees that produce the hardwoods are slow growing, which accounts for the higher price. Two of the softwoods, cedar and redwood, are slow growing but their resistance to outdoor conditions justifies the higher cost.

Lumber is usually sold by the board foot, which is the basis for the price shown on a piece of lumber. A board foot is a piece of lumber 1″ thick by 12″ wide by 12″ long. When calculating the number of board feet required for a project, multiply the board's thickness in inches by the width in inches, then by the length in feet and divide that number by twelve.

As experienced woodworkers know, stated lumber sizes are not always as they appear. For example, a 2×4 board is normally dressed kiln dried to $1\frac{1}{2}″ \times 3\frac{1}{2}″$.

There is a grading system for lumber, and you'll often see terms like "select" and "common" grades. If you're not familiar with the grading system in your area, it would be time well spent to acquire the government grading regulations brochure. Details such as defects allowed, moisture content and species are often contained in the ratings.

A tree's weight is made up of a high proportion of water. Boards just cut from the tree are very "wet," and are often referred to as "green" lumber. It's best to purchase kiln-dried lumber with a moisture content of 15 percent or less. Lumber of this type is reasonably stable since most of the shrinking is complete.

You can imagine the problems if we joined lumber with a high moisture content. Joints such as the common mortise and tenon would more than likely fail as the wood dried. But we're going to take this so-called "dry" lumber and put it outside in the rain. Here's where proper finishing is important. We want to do everything we can to preserve the wood's original state.

There are safety issues to consider when working with wood. One of them, toxic reactions to wood, should be studied by all woodworkers. Certain woods are more toxic than others and not everyone reacts to the wood in the same manner. Most libraries have books that deal with this subject and it's advisable that you read and understand the issues.

The specifications of each outdoor wood will be detailed so you can decide which type is best for your project. When you're ready to start, call two or three local lumber suppliers for a price list of the wood types.

However, we aren't limited to buying kiln-dried expensive lumber for these projects. You can use construction-grade or sawn green (also called S-green or S-GRN) wood with a bit of planning. New wood, if not kiln-dried, should have ample time to dry out. Unassembled boards should be air dried for 4 to 6 weeks in warm, dry weather. Spacers should be placed in each layer so that air can circulate and dry the wood. If rain is forecasted, cover the wood.

I know many woodworkers who build outdoor projects using "green wood." And with sufficient planning and lead time allowing the wood to dry before use, we can also use non kiln-dried wood and save quite a bit of money in the process.

CEDAR

Cedar is classified as a softwood with desirable decay-resistant properties. Generally known as western red cedar or eastern white cedar, its color ranges from a light tan to a dark red. This softwood is easy to work with and, while not exceptionally strong, it's more than acceptable for most outdoor furniture projects. In some parts of North America, it's the wood of choice for decks, picnic tables and fences.

With the exception of pressure-treated wood, cedar is the least expensive of the outdoor project woods. However, select cedar relatively free of knots and checks can be as expensive as some hardwoods in parts of the country. When pricing lumber, be certain to inquire about the grade classification. "Number one common" cedar will be drastically cheaper than "select A cedar," but there will be a drastic difference in appearance as well.

In general, cedar is a good choice. If you are able to select the wood at the lumberyard, you'll find many usable pieces of wood in the common grade. With selective picking and careful cutting, cedar will meet most of your requirements.

REDWOOD

Thirty years ago, redwood was plentiful and relatively inexpensive. Today, however, this western coastal wood is protected by the government and production is strictly controlled. It tends to be expensive and hard to get on the eastern coast of North America. If you live on the West Coast, you may still find this desirable softwood reasonably priced and therefore a good choice for your projects.

Redwood is soft and easy to work, but care must be taken to avoid splintering. It has a beautiful red color and is extremely decay-resistant. It has been the choice wood for outdoor projects and was commonly used for house siding.

More information on this wood, its properties and grading procedures as well as suggested applications is available from the California Redwood Association.

MAHOGANY

There are three commonly available types of mahogany: Honduras, African and Philippine. The first two are used in furniture construction, while the coarse, open-grained Philippine mahogany is often used for interior doors and trim work.

Decay-resistant and long-time favorites of boat-builders, Honduras and African mahogany have beautiful color and texture. They are ideal for building outdoor furniture and are often reasonably priced.

The board foot price can vary depending on your area's supply and demand. You may also find that the names are different and it's sometimes difficult to determine just what you're getting. Honduras mahogany is called "Genuine" or "Central American" in some areas. However, the goal is to buy a furniture-grade wood with properties that are found in the Honduras mahogany.

TEAK

This hardwood is also a boatbuilder's wood because of its decay- and water-resistant characteristics. Teak feels oily and has a high silica content. Therefore, carbide cutting tools are a necessity when working this wood. It ranges in color from yellow-brown to dark brown. Teak is a durable wood and dimensionally stable.

Teak in contact with metal does not cause rust, which makes it perfect for outdoor furniture. It is, however, increasingly rare and very expensive. The decision on whether or not to use teak depends on the project you're going to build. If a garden bench constructed of teak provides twenty years of useful service, that cost over that period is not hard to bear. If the bench only lasts a couple of years, then it is an expensive proposition.

Proper construction techniques, protection and on-going maintenance are issues that you should be even more aware of when using expensive woods like teak.

WHITE OAK

Boatbuilders and coopers have long favored white oak for building boats, barrels, casks and tubs. This wood is used by boatbuilders and distillers, so it's in demand. The supply cannot always meet this demand; conse-quently, white oak is very expensive.

Its sapwood is white and the heartwood is light brown. The heartwood pores are filled with a natural membrane called tylosis, which makes the white oak vir-tually impenetrable by water. White oak tends to expand when wet if not finished properly, which is why the wood was favored for making casks. Once filled with wine or spirits, the casks would not leak.

If you have access to a white oak tree lot, it would be a good choice for garden furniture as long as it was properly finished. If you have to buy it at the retail level, it may be more economical to use another hardwood.

PRESSURE-TREATED WOOD

Pressure-treated wood is becoming more popular for out-door construction projects. It's inexpensive and many manufacturers warranty the product for up to thirty years if properly installed.

Spruce, pine and fir are commonly used. The wood is dehydrated under a vacuum and impregnated with pre-servatives, leaving the fibers unpalatable for fungi and in-sects. The wood is stamped with letters designating the type of chemical applied, most often chromate copper ar-senate (CCA) and other copper arsenates and chromates.

The treated wood can be cut and fastened like any other wood, but special attention should be given to the fact that there are chemicals present. It's advisable to read the manufacturer's safety guidelines before working with this product.

Often green or tan in color, pressure-treated wood can be painted. If left "natural," most will turn a silver-gray color. Verify that the pressure-treated wood you purchase can be painted.

Three projects in this book that can be built using pressure-treated wood are the trellises, arbor and gazebo. For that matter, just about any project in this book can be successfully built using pressure-treated wood. It's up to you and simply a matter of taste. I've seen some painted pressure-treated wood projects that are beautiful.

Choosing Hardware

One major enemy of outdoor furniture is the metal fas-tener. Steel or the common zinc-plated screws react with the tannic acids in the wood, causing dark stains and streaks. I've taken apart wood decks that were full of rot and weakened by steel screws and bolts. Do not, under any circumstances, use fastening hardware made of un-protected steel, including zinc-plated hardware.

HOT-DIPPED GALVANIZED

Screws and bolts treated by the hot-dipped galvanized method are specifically designed for outdoor use. There is an electroplated galvanized process, but it doesn't seem to hold up as well as the dipped process. Zinc is used as the coating in both methods and acts as a barrier against the tannic acid in the wood.

STAINLESS STEEL

Fasteners made from iron with chrome and nickel added are known as stainless steel. They are the most rust-resistant screws and bolts available, and the most expensive.

Stainless fasteners are hard and ideally suited for out-door furniture construction. The high price can some-times be prohibitive, but using these screws will add years of life to your furniture. In that regard, they are a small investment that will pay dividends in the long run.

OUTDOOR SCREWS

In the last few years, many hardware manufacturers have introduced a line of outdoor fastening products. Green or gray screws and sometimes bronze-colored screws can commonly be found in the deck building section of many hardware stores.

Often these screws are ceramic-coated or plated with a rust preventative to delay the metal reacting with wood acids. I've used these screws on a few outdoor projects and they seem to stand up well. However, check the supply in your area, compare the cost against the stainless steel version and see if there is a substantial difference. If there is a big difference, it may be worthwhile to use the coated hardware. However, study the specification data for these products to determine if they are suitable for your application.

Choosing an Outdoor Glue

Glue, in combination with a mechanically sound joint, is the heart of your construction project. Outdoor furniture has some special considerations that must be taken into account when constructing your project.

Outdoor glues must retain their bonding properties under some adverse conditions. Water is the most destructive element these projects will face, so the adhesives must be waterproof.

In the past, the standard outdoor glues were two-part epoxy or plastic resins. A few manufacturers have developed one-part glues that are now considered acceptable general purpose adhesives for outdoor furniture projects.

ALIPHATIC RESIN GLUE

The most recent one-part glues to be introduced are the polyaliphatic resins. One, called Titebond II, has been in common use for the last few years. It's a yellow polyaliphatic resin glue that forms a Type II bond, meaning it has to pass specific water soak tests and continue to retain its shear strength. These glues are designed for use above the waterline and therefore cannot be used on boats where the joint is submersed in water.

I've used this adhesive as a general purpose outdoor glue for various furniture projects and it appears to hold up well. If you expect extremely wet conditions for continued periods of time, it may be worth considering some of the other waterproof epoxy glues. Under normal conditions, these easy-to-use, one-part glues are suitable for all your projects, and they're inexpensive compared to the two-part epoxies and resin adhesives.

POLYURETHANE GLUE

Franklin International has introduced a glue called Titebond Polyurethane Glue and the Borden Company markets its Probond brand. They're reported to be 100 percent waterproof and are a one-part, thick glue that is ideal for outdoor furniture projects.

The product is not intended for below-the-waterline or continued submersion use. It is recommended for wood, ceramics and plastic bonding. The shear strength on hard maple has been tested at over 3,500 pounds per square inch for each of these glues. This is another of the many advances in one-part outdoor glues that have been developed in the last few years. These advances have simplified the building of outdoor projects when you compare these products to the two-part epoxy systems that were the norm in the past.

PLASTIC RESIN MARINE GLUE

Normally, this adhesive is a urea formaldehyde powder that must be mixed with water. It was considered to be the "standard" glue for marine and outdoor construction projects.

Two-part resins are more difficult to use because you must mix only the amount you'll use in a reasonable length of time. In that respect, there is a wastage factor to consider compared to the ready-to-use aliphatic or polyurethane glues.

There are some drawbacks to using plastic resins, including the urea gas given off while the glue is curing. Additionally, they cure at room temperature, so you need a heated shop.

Like many adhesives, plastic resins don't fill gaps very well, so joints must be well-fitted. Oily woods such as teak don't bond well with plastic resin.

EPOXY RESIN

When a high-strength, highly waterproof bond is needed, epoxy resin is the adhesive of choice. Most manufacturers sell a two-part system consisting of a resin and hardener.

However, epoxy resin can be frustrating to use. For all of its positive aspects, including high shear strength and almost completely waterproof properties, it has some negative aspects that must be considered.

Epoxy cures fast. If there is glue squeezed out while you are fitting the joints, it has to be removed immediately or it's there for good. Make sure not to get any on your shop equipment, including wood clamps that are temporarily holding the joint, because it won't come off easily. The price for epoxy resin can also be high: A 40-ounce kit can cost as much as $40.

CONSTRUCTION ADHESIVES

Over the last few years, I've used some of the latest exterior construction adhesives. They are sold in cans or caulking gun tubes. In general, I've found them to be more than satisfactory for many outdoor building projects. I normally use adhesives that are available in tubes for use with my caulking gun because they are simple to apply. Look for the best ratings possible and follow the manufacturer's instructions. These paste adhesives are easy to apply and inexpensive when compared to some of the other exterior glues.

MAKING THE GLUE CHOICE

When considering all the glues available today, I've opted for the polyurethane glues or the exterior construction adhesive. There are some disadvantages in that they don't have the high waterproof ratings of the resin and epoxy glues. But for general purpose outdoor furniture under normal conditions, these one-part glues and construction adhesives are more than acceptable. They've progressed a great deal in the last few years.

For your own peace of mind, look at the general weather conditions in your area and study the adhesive's ratings applicable to those conditions. In most cases, the one-part glues will serve your purposes.

Finishing Outdoor Projects

Concern for the environment has forced many manufacturers to develop more "environmentally friendly" exterior wood finishes. Because the laws differ from region to region, it's difficult to recommend one all-around finish. As weather conditions vary in each area, so does the concern for the level of protection required.

Many regions have laws limiting the volatile organic compounds (VOC) given off by exterior wood coatings. Due to these new laws, manufacturers are developing new products to meet the standards. The changes are rapid and numerous, so keeping track of the new coatings available is a difficult job.

No matter where you live, one problem you'll encounter is discoloration of the wood. Ultraviolet light (radiation) breaks down the surface cells in the lumber and turns most species gray. Therefore, you need a finish that has a UV blocker to maintain the wood's natural color. That's the first issue.

Secondly, no matter what product you use, refinishing every few years will be necessary. I don't believe there's an exterior finish made that will last more than five years under the most ideal conditions.

There are two main categories of exterior finishes: penetrating stains and surface coatings. However, recent environmental legislation has caused manufacturers to try new formulas. There are water-based and water-oil-modified formulations as well as an attempt to increase the solids in an oil-based coating.

One general rule for exterior wood finishes is to try to use a penetrating stain. Surface coatings, such as paint or varnish, will eventually blister and peel. While penetrating stains fade and become weathered, they don't blister. It's simpler to sand and refinish stained wood because you don't have to scrape and sand blistered coatings. There are many exterior penetrating finishes on the market. They are often called water-repellent exterior stains or wood protectors.

To enhance the natural color of the wood, use a clear finish. If you want to change the color of the wood slightly while enhancing the grain, use a transparent or semitransparent exterior stain.

FINISHING DO'S AND DONT'S

Try to apply all finishes when the temperature is between 10°C/50°F and 35°C/95°F. Temperatures that are either too hot or cold can have a negative effect on the final finish.

Be certain to saturate all end grains, and apply liberal coats of finish to the wood. Try and maintain a "wet edge" when using any finish, and coat in the direction of the grain.

Do not apply finishes in direct sunlight or when the surface is hot to the touch. If there is dew or frost present, many stains will not work properly. Applying any coating in wet weather will result in a very poor finish and you may trap moisture in the wood.

As a general rule, I suggest that you do not apply any finishes to wood that has a moisture content higher than 18 percent.

There are many manufacturers in the marketplace,

and most have very good products. Read the literature offered by these companies and study their warranty programs. If possible, find someone who has used a finish you like on outdoor furniture to determine how it's held up to local weather conditions.

SANDING/FINISHING TIPS

Here are a few sanding and finishing tips that may improve the looks of your project.

- Sanding should be done as close to wood finishing as possible.
- The coarser the sandpaper grit used, the darker the stain color produced due to penetration.
- Use caution when working with a belt sander: A worn belt will polish the wood surface. Worn belts can also cause intense heat that will burn the wood, which may restrict finish penetration.
- To avoid scratches, use a series of grits with the next grit only one grade finer than the previous. For example, a sanding sequence could be 100, 120 and finally 140.
- Sanding new wood should be done with an open-coat type paper made with silicone carbide or aluminum oxide. Silicon papers should be used for sanding between finishes.
- Sanding not only smooths the wood, it prepares the wood for finish by creating an anchor for the coating.

Joinery Techniques Used in the Book

It isn't my intention to teach wood joinery in this book. Volumes could be written on this subject alone. *Good Wood Joints* by Albert Jackson and David Day is an excellent resource on wood joinery. However, I will detail the joinery with each project.

Most experienced woodworkers have made many of the joints used throughout this book. Lap, mortise-and-tenon, dowel and dado joints are a few of the methods of joining wood that we'll use. In general, the mortise-and-tenon joint or one of its many variations will be featured and used extensively when building the projects.

MORTISE-AND-TENON JOINTS

This joint has been used as the standard method of attaching two pieces of wood for centuries. It's most often used to attach wood at right angles.

This joint gets its mechanical strength from one piece of wood being fitted into another and joined with glue and fasteners. There are many variations of the mortise and tenon and as many rules for joint sizes.

One rule many people follow is that the thickness of the tenon should equal one third the width of the stock. For example, two 1½" pieces of wood, joined at right angles, will have a ½" tenon.

For the majority of applications, leaving a ⅛" shoulder around the tenon and then making the mortise to fit normally provides a solid, mechanically sound joint. The joint should fit securely but still allow room for glue. If you have to hammer the mortise and tenon together, it's too tight.

These joints can be cut by hand, on a table saw and drill press or with a table saw and mortise drill press equipped with a mortising chisel. It doesn't matter how you make the joint as long as it's secure.

DADO JOINTS

Dado joints are best cut with either a router or carbide dado blade assembly on a table saw. They are a simple joint to make and one that most everyone has mastered.

This joint is a slot that joins two pieces of wood, often at right angles. As with all other joints, it should be snug without binding.

BISCUIT JOINTS

Over the last few years, biscuit joinery has gained tremendous popularity. Biscuit joiners allow the woodworker to make a quick, clean, accurate joint. A biscuit cut from beech wood is inserted into the slot and when glue is applied, the biscuit swells, tightening the bond.

Biscuit joinery has many applications but is well suited to strengthening miter joints. It is also good for butt joinery, particularly for panel glue-ups.

The cutting tool called a biscuit joiner is reasonably priced. Most woodworkers will find that this tool is a handy addition to their shop.

OTHER JOINERY

As discussed earlier, there are numerous joints used throughout this book. However, none are extremely complicated. A little care and attention when cutting these joints will result in success every time.

If you're intimidated by any woodworking procedures in this book, practice on the simpler projects. Most projects in total look difficult. Breaking them down into smaller sections always simplifies the process. Practice the joinery on scrap lumber and you'll soon master all of the procedures. As my wise cabinetmaker father often said, "It's only a few sticks of wood glued together, making it look complicated." Concentrate on the individual sections and the whole project will come together successfully.

Other Outdoor Furniture Options

Now, after going through all the wood types and finishing principles, I'm going to contradict myself. I believe that you can use any wood outside with success, but that statement is heavily weighted with a precaution: The wood must be properly protected.

To illustrate my point, I've used pine outdoors on many occasions and those structures are still serving me well. How do you achieve these successful results? Simply make certain that all wood surfaces are coated with a protective wood preservative.

Protecting all surfaces means using a clear wood preservative after all of the parts are cut to size, but prior to joining. In many cases, rot caused by moisture and mildew happens at the spot where two boards are joined. This is where there is often a lack of air circulation, and the wood on the joint surfaces is left unprotected. Bare wood, no matter the species, won't stand up long under these conditions. I agree that some woods, such as teak, are naturally resistant, but a little extra insurance is always the best policy. Make it a practice to use a clear protective coating on all surfaces and you'll extend the wood's life greatly. Applying a little extra to the joint areas as well will go a long way to help prevent damage.

One of the owners of the lumberyard where I purchase much of my wood strongly recommends the protective coatings. He often uses pine in place of cedar outdoors because it "holds" a screw or fastener better, resulting in a stronger joint. It's not always a cost issue because he has all the wood species available.

When using pine for outdoor structures, cut and sand all parts. Liberally apply a clear wood preservative to all surfaces, but be certain the wood's moisture content is below 18 percent. Assemble the project, then coat with a protective translucent finish for exterior wood. You can use any quality finish such as the Sikkens or Olympic products.

There are many pleasing colors available. You can use a mahogany finish on pine with dramatic results. As always, test the finishes completely before committing to the final coat.

Most clear protective exterior penetrating finishes allow you to apply a stained finish. But it's worth repeating: Make sure all of the products are compatible.

I'll detail the finish on each project and will use various woods and stains to illustrate the different combinations. Your choice of which one to use is a matter of personal taste, but the protection process is mandatory if you want many years of enjoyable service from the outdoor projects you create.

CHAPTER 3

Elegant Dining Set

Nothing beats the feeling of enjoying a great meal outdoors with family and friends. To complement that setting, I'll detail the plans for building an elegant dining table and chairs. Throughout this book I will be using different species of woods for the projects. For the dining set I chose birch because of its hardness and durability. There was quite a lot of birch left over in the shop from various kitchen cabinet and furniture projects. Some pieces were rejected because of color or defects. However, they were ideal for this table and chairs, as most of the project uses ¾″-thick material glued up for the table and chair leg assemblies.

Can you use thick wood for these projects? By all means, substitute solid wood for the glue-ups if you have the material. But if you have a surplus of 1″ planks that are less than perfect, this application is ideal.

Dining Table

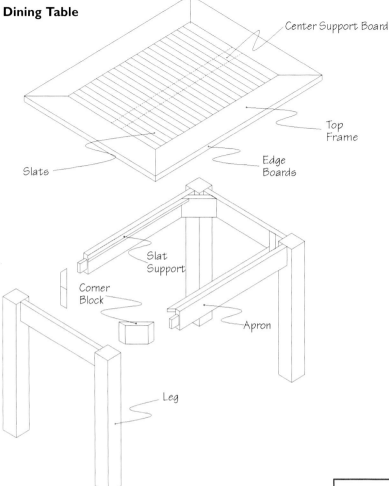

Center Support Board

Top Frame

Slats

Edge Boards

Slat Support

Corner Block

Apron

Leg

Designing the Dining Set

The table is strong and comfortably seats four people. The chairs are a straight-backed style that many find comfortable when dining. However, about half the people who visited the shop during construction said they preferred a chair back that was tipped backwards. The choice is yours, and I suggest you mock up a chair before committing to the final design. The most common backward slant on chairs is 10°–15°. To achieve a tipped-back chair style, simply glue up wider stock and cut out the backs much like we will do with the garden bench in chapter four.

You'll have to alter a couple of dimensions, such as the chair arm length, but they're minor adjustments.

Table		
Number	**Part**	**Dimensions** (**Thickness** × **Width** × **Length**)
4	Legs	3″ × 3″ × 28¾″
4	Apron	¾″ × 3″ × 36″
4	Corner Blocks	¾″ × 3″ × 5″
4	Top Frame	¾″ × 6½″ × 47″
4	Edge Boards	¾″ × 1½″ × 47″
2	Slat Supports	¾″ × 2″ × 33″
13	Slats	¾″ × 2½ × 34″

In order to get these parts, you will need to find or purchase the following lumber and supplies:

Number	**Nominal Stock Size**	**To Yield These Parts**
12	1″ × 6″ × 10′	Chair Legs
4	1″ × 4″ × 10′	Table Legs
6	1″ × 2″ × 8′	Chair Bottom Back Rails, Cross Rails, Rail Stretchers, Built-up Edge Boards
6	1″ × 4″ × 8′	Chair Top Back Rails, Front Seat Support Rails, Seat Rails, Table Apron
7	1″ × 3″ × 8′	Back Seat Support Rails, Seat Slats, Arms
5	1″ × 3″ × 10′	Table Slat Supports, Table Slats
2	1″ × 8″ × 8′	Tabletop Perimeter

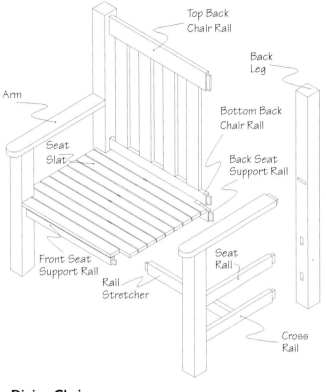

Dining Chair

Chair

Cutting list represents one chair—multiply by number of chairs for accurate bill of materials

Number	Part	Dimensions (Thickness × Width × Length)
2	Front Legs	2¼″ × 2¼″ × 24″
2	Back Legs	2¼″ × 2¼″ × 33″
1	Bottom Back Chair Rail	¾″ × 1½″ × 21″
1	Top Back Chair Rail	¾″ × 3″ × 21″
1	Back Seat Support Rail	¾″ × 1¾″ × 21″
1	Front Seat Support Rail	¾″ × 3″ × 21″
2	Cross Rails	¾″ × 1½″ × 18″
2	Seat Rails	¾″ × 3″ × 18″
1	Rail Stretcher	¾″ × 1½″ × 21″
2	Arms	¾″ × 2⅝″ × 20″
5	Back Slats	⅜″ × 1½″ × 13⅝″
4	Center Back Spacers	⅜″ × ¼″ × 1⅞″
4	End Back Spacers	⅜″ × ¼″ × 2″
7	Seat Slats	¾″ × 2⅝″ × 23¼″

Estimating Cost and Value

The cost of material for this project is by no means insignificant. If you're buying kiln-dried hardwood from a retail lumberyard, you'd better have a strong cup of coffee before looking at the price tag. In terms of cost and quality, consider for a moment the ready-made sets that are being offered. Most are not well built and the price is often high. The joinery isn't great, the quality of the wood leaves a lot to be desired, and if the commercial set is made from hardwood, it's not always easy to match some of the pieces you've previously built.

Value—in terms of good wood, proper fasteners and glue, a good finish and quality workmanship—is not always found in commercially made outdoor dining sets. Build this project with the best materials and finishes available and it will last twenty years or more. Spread the investment over that many years and the cost is very reasonable. As the saying goes, "Buy the best and cry once; buy cheap and cry twice." It makes good economic sense in this instance.

The Final Product

Take time to decide on the final chair and table design. Use high-quality material, fit and fasten all the joints with care and you'll have a unique dining set that will last years into the future. Then relax, invite a few friends for dinner on the deck and begin enjoying this elegant woodworking project.

Construction Steps

1 Cut and glue up eight front leg assemblies (if building four chairs) by joining three boards at ¾″ × 2½″ × 25″ for each leg for a total of 24 boards. After the glue has set, plane and trim each of the eight legs to 2¼″ × 2¼″ × 24″ long. If you plan on using thick stock, dress each leg to the finished size.

2 In the same manner, glue up eight rear leg assemblies using 24 boards at ¾″ × 2½″ × 34″. Dress to a finished size of 2¼″ × 2¼″ × 33″.

3 While the clamps and glue are available, form the table leg assemblies. These four legs each require four boards at ¾″ × 3¼″ × 29¼″. Sixteen boards are needed to form the rough legs. Dress to a finished size of 3″ × 3″ × 28¾″.

4 Mark up the mortises and tenons for the front legs as shown in the diagram. All tenons and their corresponding mortises are ½″ wide unless otherwise noted.

5 Mark up the position of the mortises and tenons for the rear leg assemblies as shown in "Mortise and Tenon Position of Rear Leg Assembly."

Step 4

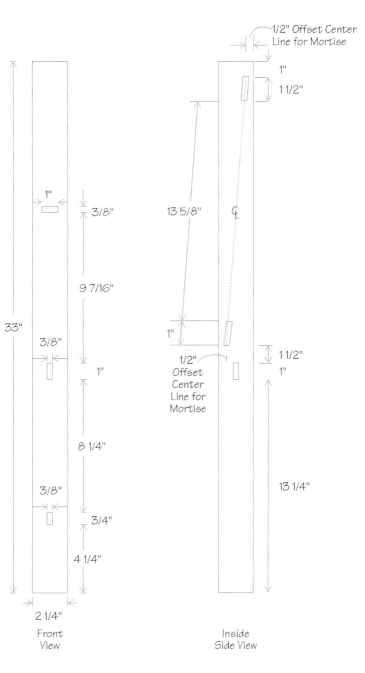

Mortise and Tenon Position of Rear Leg Assembly

Front View

Inside Side View

6 It's easiest to temporarily clamp parts together when marking multiple, identical pieces. However, be careful as there is a "right" and "left" leg for each chair with both the front and rear assemblies.

7 Form the mortises and tenons on the front legs as well as the mortises on the rear legs.

8 The tenons on the front legs can be cut on a table saw or with a handsaw and chisel.

9 Clean mortises, sand legs and round over all of the edges with a ¼″ roundover router bit. Additionally, round over the bottom ends of the front legs and the top and bottom ends of the rear legs.

10 Cut the chair back bottom rail as shown and form the tenons on each end.

11 The chair top back rail is curved at the top edge. Before forming the curve, cut the tenons on each end as shown in "Chair—Top Back Rail."

12 The curve layout on the rail is simply a straight line from the center of the rail to a point 2½″ up from the bottom on each end of the rail.

13 Cut the four chair upper rail back curves. Clamp the four boards together and sand to form an identical, even curve on all the pieces.

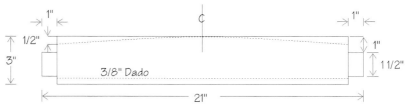

Chair–Top Back Rail

Step 8

Step 9

Step 12

Step 13

Choosing a Glue
In this project, a moisture-cured, polyurethane expanding glue such as TiteBond or Probond is the best adhesive to use.

14 Plow a ⅜" dado in the bottom, centered on the edge, of the top chair rail and the top of the bottom rail to receive the back slats.

15 Using a ¼" roundover bit in a router, ease the top edge of the top chair rail (see "Chair—Top Back Rail"), and the bottom edge of the bottom chair rail.

16 Dry fit chair backs to ensure the joints are secure and properly positioned.

17 Cut five back slats per chair at ⅜" thick by 1½" wide by 13⅝" long. You will also need eight spacers per chair at ⅜" thick by ¼" high by 1⅞" wide that will separate the slats. The first and last spacer on the top and bottom will be cut at 2" wide to completely fill the space (see "Chair—Back Layouts"). Dry fit and check the fit of the slats, spacers and rails.

18 Four rear seat supports must be cut and tenoned before finally assembling the chair backs. The rail measures ¾" × 1¾" × 21" long.

19 Once you verify that all chair back parts are correctly cut, glue and assemble all the parts.

20 Prepare four front seat support rails from ¾" stock. Verify the fit and join the front chair assemblies. Round over the outside bottom edge of the rail with a ¼" bit. Pay attention to the leg orientation with respect to its final position as part of the chair before committing it to glue.

21 Prepare two cross rail boards from ¾" stock for each chair. Dry fit the front and rear chair assemblies to each other using two cross rails per chair as shown. Do not glue until the seat rails are ready to be installed. Round over the outside edges, both upper and lower.

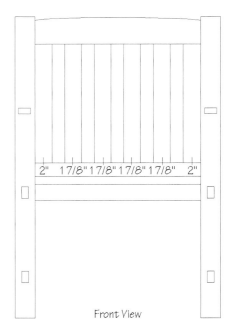

Front View

Chair—Back Layout

Step 21

Glue-up Shortcut
Gang the boards together when gluing up chair and table legs. In this way, only a few clamps are needed for each series of legs.

22 The curved seat rails are cut from ¾″ stock beginning at 3″ wide by 18″ long. Cut both tenons as shown referencing the back tenon from the bottom edge. The slope for the seat begins 7″ from the front and gradually tapers the rail to the back at a point 1¾″ from the bottom edge of the rail as shown in "Curved Seat Rail." Cut all seat rails with this taper, and clamp together for the final sanding and forming. We want to achieve a nice, gentle "S" slope for the seat slats. This will ensure that all of the parts are identical.

23 Once these seat rails have been dry fit and are correct, the chair front and back assemblies can be glued to each other with the cross rails and seat rails. Attach the four rails to the back section first, then join the front assembly. Make certain all of the parts are oriented correctly before applying adhesive. Cut a straight piece of wood from ¾″ stock for each chair and install in the cross rail dadoes. Glue and clamp where necessary.

24 Cut seven seat slats for each chair at ¾″ × 2⅝″ × 23¼″. The front and rear seat slat for each chair is notched to fit around the legs. We want to have a ¼″ overhang of the slat over the seat support at both front and rear. Drill and countersink the slat so that we can attach it to the rails with 2″ exterior screws. Fill the ⅜″ countersunk holes with a wood plug.

25 Attach the remaining five slats in the same manner with about ¼″ spacing.

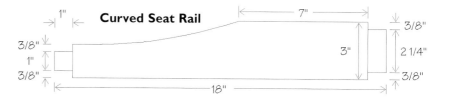

Curved Seat Rail

Step 22

Step 24

Step 25

Chair–Arm Layout

Round over corners

2 5/8"

Mortise to fit

1"
13/16"
1"
13/16"

20"

26 Secure all seat slats with glue and screws. Fill the holes with a wood plug and sand the plugs flush.

27 Two arms are required for each chair to complete the assembly. Cut as shown in "Chair—Arm Layout." The chair arms are cut from ¾" stock. The tenon is ⅜" thick and 1" wide.

28 Round over all the corners with a belt sander. Clamp each pair of chair arms together when sanding so they'll be identical.

29 Gently fit each arm's rear tenon into its mortise. Center the arm on the front leg tenon and trace the mortise outline on the bottom of each arm. Reference each arm position with a mark so that you'll be able to return to the side where the mortise was outlined.

30 Once the mortise has been cut, glue and clamp each in place. Let the glue set up for at least four hours while clamped.

31 We can now turn our attention to the table. The dressed size of the four legs is 3" × 3" × 28¾". Verify the finished size and sand all surfaces of the legs.

Step 29

Step 32

Step 33

Avoiding Splinters

Rounding over chair and table leg bottoms eliminates sharp corners, which may splinter when the furniture is moved on a hard surface such as a stone patio.

32 Cut two mortises in each leg as shown in "Table—Leg Mortise Layout." Ease all the corners of the legs with a ¼" roundover bit.

33 Next we require four apron boards that are each ¾" × 3" × 36" and have a tenon on each end as shown.

34 Assemble the four aprons and table legs using glue and securing with long pipe clamps.

35 To add strength at the leg to the apron joint, a corner block is attached with screws and glue.

36 The tabletop perimeter is simply four boards joined at 45°. The joints are secured with biscuits and glue. Each piece has an overall length of 47" and is 6½" wide by ¾" thick. Prepare as shown in "Tabletop Perimeter."

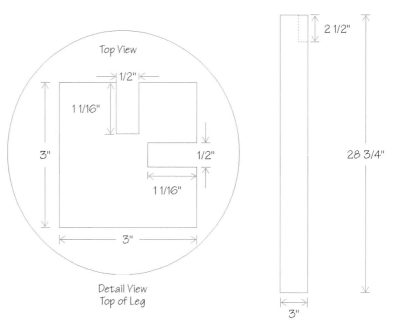

Table—Leg Mortise Layout

Step 35

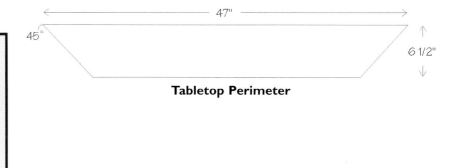

Tabletop Perimeter

Making Identical Parts

Forming multiple, identical furniture parts is common to many projects in this book. The easiest way to achieve uniformity of parts is to clamp them all together and then complete the final sanding process.

37 Install the biscuits, then glue and clamp each joint as shown.

38 To increase the edge thickness of the table, glue and screw four boards, as shown in "Table—Edge Boards," to the underside of the table. The added boards are installed flush with the outside edge.

39 Two table slat support boards must be installed on opposite sides. The length of these support boards may vary a little because of the placement of the corner blocks. It's best to lay the boards in position and mark as shown.

40 Attach the slat support boards with glue and screws as shown.

Step 38

47"   45°   1 1/2"

Table—Edge Boards

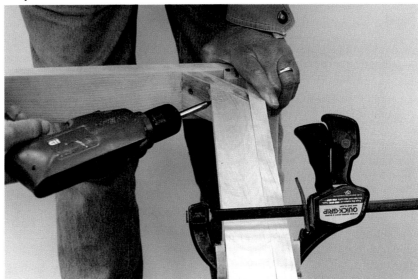

Step 39

Equal Spacing Tip

Lay all of the slats on the chair rails to determine the required—and equal—spacing between each member.

Step 40

41 On the frame edges, opposite to the slat support boards, install tabletop attachment blocks. The size is not critical, but a block ¾″ thick by 1″ wide and 3″ long was found to be more than sufficient to secure the tabletop perimeter.

42 Secure the tabletop perimeter frame with one screw through each support block and two through each slat support.

43 Before installing the table slats, sand and round over the tabletop edges, both top and bottom, with a ½″ roundover bit.

44 Thirteen table slats at ¾″ × 2½″ × 34″ are required. The spacing is approximately ¹⁄₁₆″ and is determined by dry fitting and adjusting all of the slats in their final position. When the spacing is determined, attach the slats with glue and screws from the underside. Carefully install 1¼″ screws in pilot holes so the screw doesn't come through the top.

45 Install a center support board, with a screw in each slat, along the center line of the table to maintain the level from board to board. This board is ¾″ thick by 2½″ wide and long enough to attach to all of the table slats.

46 One final sanding and the table is ready for finishing.

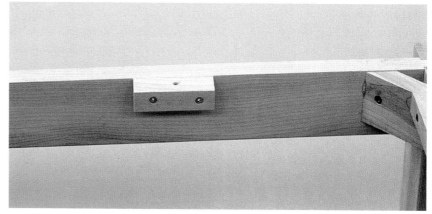

Step 41

Step 42

Step 45

Construction Notes

This outdoor dining set is not difficult to construct, but it does require a good deal of lumber and tests your skill forming the joints. However, time and patience go a long way toward the successful completion of this project.

As was stated in the introduction, some people prefer a chair back that has a 10° or 15° slant. It would be well worth your while to mock up a chair to determine your preference.

Pay special attention to the environment where this table will be used. If the conditions are wet, make sure all of the areas where water and moisture can collect are provided with adequate drainage. Drill holes for water runoff in areas such as the intersection of the center slat support board and the table slats. If you do provide drainage holes, give the hole a little extra protection with additional paint. Check these holes periodically to ensure they aren't clogged.

The table and chairs had three coats of Sikkens Cetol 1 #078 Natural stain, which produces a slight orange tone. Any good outdoor stain will protect the wood as long as the coating is applied properly.

Variations and Options

Birch was used for this project, but it's easily built with almost any wood. Some of the more expensive woods such as teak and mahogany are excellent alternatives.

The table is 4′ square but you can build it to any size that's required. The same construction principles apply to a table 4′ × 6′. Simply alter the dimensions and follow the steps.

Slat spacing was set at about ¹⁄₁₆″ because this table will be used outdoors. If you plan to have this set on a covered porch or in a sunroom, slat spacing can be reduced or a glued-up solid top could be installed.

It's also possible to create an oval table by using wider perimeter boards and cutting the pattern you desire. If you decide on an oval or round style, pay attention to the biscuit placement at the corners. First draw the pattern for the top, then align the biscuits inside the perimeter.

The glued-up chair and table legs can be made from solid wood if you have access to thicker stock material. In fact, it may be a worthwhile exercise to compare the price of material in your area.

All in all, this dining set is a challenging, yet satisfying woodworking project that should provide many years of useful service.

Getting Tight Joints

Temporarily attach two clamping blocks per corner on the underside of the table. Line up these blocks so they are parallel with the joint and draw the joint firmly together with a C-clamp.

CHAPTER 4

Classic Garden Bench

Often, one of the most desired pieces of outdoor furniture is a garden bench. Many of us have just the ideal spot for this project: on the front porch so we can watch the world rush by, on the backyard deck or even tucked away in a secluded spot as part of the garden setting.

During my research for the ideal bench, I looked at some of the commercial offerings at my home store. Many were light-duty models made out of pine or cedar. The high-end commercial models, made from teak and mahogany, would certainly have put my budget in a tailspin.

How do we get the quality of those high-end commercial models without considering a second mortgage on our homes? Well, as woodworkers, we have the option to build the project ourselves with substantial savings and, most

likely, at a higher quality. First decide on the basic design and then choose the construction materials.

After looking at many styles, I decided to design and build a garden bench that is considered more North American in design. The English style seemed to have thin legs, curved arms and delicate lines. The American style tended to be heavier in appearance with thick legs and flat, wide arms. It made a strong visual statement.

The garden bench in this chapter is truly a North American classic with heavy, 3″-square legs and thick, 1½″ arms. Stringers and seat slats also continue the theme as they are constructed out of 1½″-thick material.

There are many woods to choose from and, because I wanted a bench that would last for years, I decided to use a hardwood. Ash is a hardwood used in the cabinetmaking

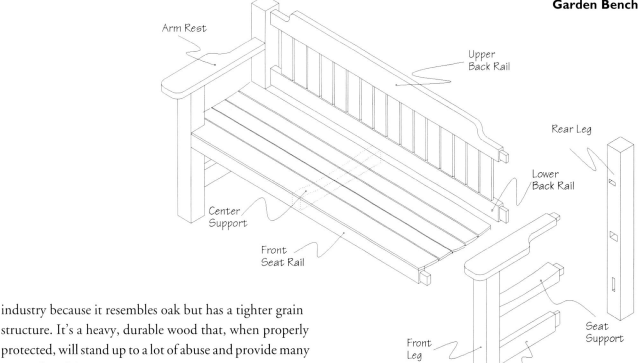

Arm Rest

Upper
Back Rail

Rear Leg

Lower
Back Rail

Center
Support

Front
Seat Rail

Seat
Support

Front
Leg

Lower
Leg Rail

industry because it resembles oak but has a tighter grain structure. It's a heavy, durable wood that, when properly protected, will stand up to a lot of abuse and provide many years of useful service.

Mortise-and-tenon joinery is used throughout this project since it's an ideal joint to connect many of the right-angle intersections. And waterproof polyurethane glue proved to be an excellent choice for all of these joints.

Once again, I opted to "create" the thick material for the legs by gluing 1½″ boards together. This method was ideal as I needed 5½″-wide by 3″-thick wood blanks for the curved rear legs. All of the other pieces for this bench are no more than 1½″ thick.

As we discussed in chapter three, achieving the best combination of seat curve and back slant with chairs is often difficult. We want a chair that's comfortable for everyone, but we are not all the same shape and size. This bench design proved to be very comfortable with its curved seat and slanted back. I believe the ideal combination of these two important features was achieved. However, you may want to mock up the seat curve and back slant before committing to the final design.

Filling Voids in Wood

If the wood is cracked from poor air-drying, as was the case with the ash I was using, fill the voids with polyurethane glue and a little sawdust. You'll be able to sand the area when the glue sets and eliminate a place where water can penetrate.

Garden Bench

Number	Part	Dimensions (Thickness × Width × Length)
2	Front Legs	3″ × 3″ × 23¼″
2	Rear Legs	3″ × 3″ × 32½″
1	Upper Back Rail	1½″ × 5½″ × 68″
1	Lower Back Rail	1½″ × 3″ × 68″
1	Front Seat Rail	1½″ × 3″ × 68″
2	Lower Leg Rails	1½″ × 3″ × 18″
2	Seat Supports	1½″ × 3″ × 18″
1	Center Support	1½″ × 2¼″ × 16¼″
14	Back Slats	¾″ × 2¼″ × 14″
26	Slat Spacers	½″ × ¾″ × 2¼″
4	End Slat Spacers	½″ × ¾″ × 2⅛″
5	Seat Boards	1½″ × 2¾″ × 71″
1	Front Seat Board	1½″ × 2¾″ × 65″
2	Armrests	1½″ × 5½″ × 21″

In order to get these parts, you will need to find or purchase the following lumber and supplies:

Number	Nominal Stock Size	To Yield These Parts
9	2″ × 4″ × 8′	Front Legs, Lower Back Rail, Front Seat Rail, Lower Leg Rail, Seat Support, Seat Slats
3	2″ × 6″ × 8′	Rear Legs, Upper Back Rail, Armrest
2	1″ × 3″ × 10′	Back Slats

Construction Steps

1 The front and rear legs are formed by gluing up 1½"-thick boards. Four pieces are needed for the two front legs. Each leg requires two boards at 1½" × 3" × 24". Each of the two rear leg blanks are formed by gluing two 1½" × 5¼" × 34" boards as shown. Use moisture cured polyurethane glue for each of the blanks.

2 Dress the front legs to a finished size of 3" × 3" × 23¼".

3 Form a tenon on one end of each front leg assembly as shown in "Front Leg Mortises."

4 Next, mark and cut the mortises on the front legs, also shown in "Front Leg Mortises."

5 Sand the front legs and soften the edges with a ¼" roundover bit in a router.

6 Lay out the curved back leg assemblies on the 3" × 5¼" × 34" wood blanks as shown in "Back Leg Layout."

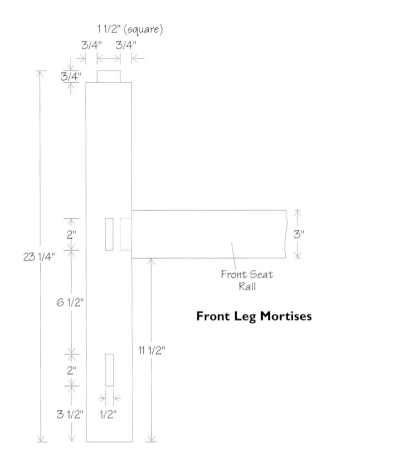

Front Leg Mortises

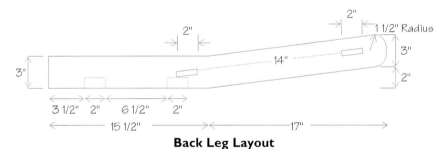

Back Leg Layout

Step 6

Step 7

7 Using a band saw is the easiest way to cut the back legs. However, it's possible to use a jigsaw that has a fairly long travel distance if you haven't got access to a band saw. After cutting, clamp the legs together and sand so they will be the same size.

8 Form the mortises in the rear legs. Prior to cutting them, verify that their position is the same on both back and front legs for the seat supports and leg rails.

9 The back assembly must be inserted into the rear legs prior to attaching the front and rear sections of the bench. First, we need an upper back rail that has overall dimensions of $1\frac{1}{2}'' \times 5\frac{1}{2}'' \times 68''$, cut as shown in "Upper Back Rail." I created a curved template by marking lines parallel to each other, spaced 1″ apart over an 8″ run. Beginning at 3″ from the bottom, I marked a point on each line ⅜″ higher than the last. This slight upward curved template allowed me to mark the rail slope, starting at 10″ from each rail end.

10 Cut the curve using a jigsaw and sand.

11 Next, cut a lower back rail measuring $1\frac{1}{2}'' \times 3'' \times 68''$.

12 Using a router with a ½″ straight cutting bit or a table saw equipped with a dado blade, plow a ¾″-wide by ½″-deep dado in the center of the upper back rail lower side and top side of the bottom back rail (see "Dado for Upper and Lower Back Rails"). These dadoes will accept the ¾″-thick back slats.

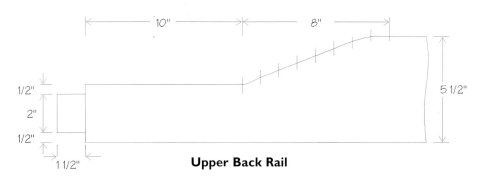

Upper Back Rail

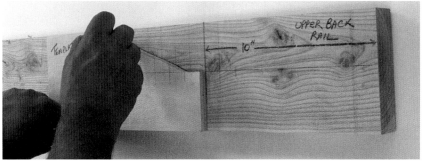

Step 9

Step 12

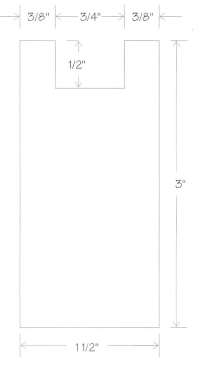

Dado for Upper and Lower Back Rails

Cutting Tight Mortise-and-Tenon Joints

Mortises can be cut in many ways. If you have a dedicated square chisel mortiser, it's an easy process. If you haven't got access to one of these machines, a drill press will allow you to make excellent round-corner mortises. The tenon corners can be rounded over with a wood file for a tight fit.

13 Form the two ½″-thick by 1½″-deep by 2″-long tenons on each end of the upper and lower back rails.

14 Prepare 14 back slats at ¾″ thick by 2¼″ wide by 14″ long. You will also need to cut 26 slat spacers at ½″ × ¾″ × 2¼″ long. Four spacers at ½″ × ¾″ × 2⅛″ long are also needed. These shorter pieces are the first and last spacers on the upper and lower rails.

15 Insert the spacers and slats into the upper and lower back rails. Beginning at one end, insert a 2⅛″ spacer with glue and a small brad nail from behind to hold the spacer until the glue sets. Remember to use galvanized brads. Next, install a slat, then a 2¼″ spacer and so on. Work on the upper and lower rail, securing each spacer and slat as they are installed until all of the parts are attached. The last piece on each rail is the 2⅛″ spacer. Assemble the back to the rear legs.

16 A front seat rail to join the two front legs is required. This rail measures 1½″ × 3″ × 68″ and has a tenon on each end. Round over the bottom edge.

17 Attach the two front legs to the front seat rail. If available, use an 8′ pipe clamp to secure the assembly until the glue dries.

18 Cut two lower leg rails at 1½″ × 3″ × 18″. Each end of these rails has a tenon at ½″ thick by 1½″ deep by 2″ long. After cutting the tenons, round over all edges with a ¼″ roundover bit in a router. Test fit the joints and reference each with a witness mark for later assembly.

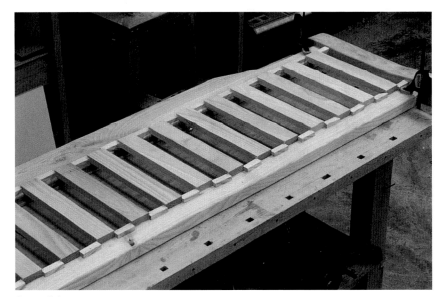

Step 14

19 We now need two seat supports that are exact copies of the lower rails. However, we will scribe and cut a curve for the seat slats in the next step. These supports are initially cut at 1½″ × 3″ × 18″ with two tenons at ½″ thick by 1½″ deep by 2″ long. After forming the tenons, reduce the depth of each by ¼″ to clear the intersecting joint of the front seat rail and lower back support rail.

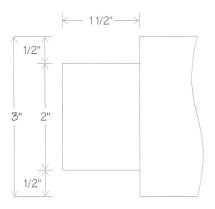

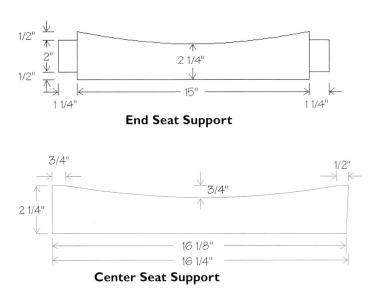

End Seat Support

Center Seat Support

20 Mark a point at the center of the seat support 2¼″ up from the bottom. Using a stick compass with a 36″ radius, draw a curve as shown in "End Seat Support." Cut both supports using a band saw or jigsaw. Clamp the two pieces together and sand smooth.

21 Round over the bottom edges of the seat supports.

22 Attach the front and rear assemblies with the lower leg rails and the seat supports. Glue and clamp in position.

23 Because the seat boards span almost 6′, a center support rail will be installed. This rail is first cut at 1½″ × 2¼″ × 16¼″ long as shown in "Center Seat Support." We want to duplicate the seat support curve, so we'll begin the radius line ¾″ in from the front to a point that is ½″ short of the back edge. The back is also angled to meet the lower back rail. Lay a straightedge from seat support to seat support to determine the correct position of the center support board. Attach the center support with glue and screws. Counterbore the screw holes and insert wood plugs.

24 Cut six seat boards. Five are 1½″ thick by 2¾″ wide by 71″ long and the sixth, which is the front board, is trimmed to 65″ long to fit between the front legs. Sand and round over the top edges.

Step 20

Step 22

Step 23

Fitting Strong Joints

Cut the mortise first. Then, using a file, form the slightly oversized tenons until they fit snugly into their respective mortises. This procedure insures strong joints.

25 Space the seat boards at ¼″ starting from the rear. This spacing will force the front seat board to overhang the front seat rail. Attach the seat boards using one 2″ screw per seat support rail, for a total of three screws per board. The front board has five 2″ screws with the two extra screws placed between the center and outside seat supports. Fill the counterbored holes with a wood plug and sand flush.

26 The arm rest is formed from a board 1½″ thick by 5½″ wide by 21″ long. Lay out the pattern on the board as shown in "Arm Rest Layout" and cut the arm.

27 The arm rest is slightly angled where it meets the back leg. I found my angle to be 8°; however, it's best to determine the angle for your bench. Lay a level board across the front leg on the shoulder beside the tenon. Mark a line on the board where the back leg intersects. Measure the angle and cut each arm rest. Make sure you place the arm correctly when cutting the angle as you are creating a right and left side.

28 Next, place each arm in its final position on top of the leg tenon and mark the mortise outline. There will be a slight error in the mortise position because the arm is not in its final position (it's higher by the height of the tenon). Take this error into account when cutting the mortise. The arm will move slightly forward in the final home position after the mortise is completed.

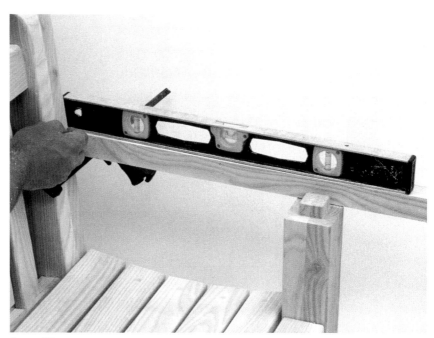

Step 27

Step 30

29 After completing the mortise and verifying that the fit is correct, sand and round over the upper and lower surfaces of both arms. Round over the front curve but do not round over the angled end.

30 Drill two countersunk pocket holes on the underside of each arm in the end where the arm meets the rear leg. Pilot drill these holes so

they exit in the middle of the arm's back end. Apply glue to the mortise as well as the back surface of the arm and attach with two 2½″ screws through the pocket holes. Clamp the front joint.

31 Your classic garden bench is now ready for final sanding and finishing.

Construction Notes

I tested various methods of attaching the arm to the rear legs. Using a mortise and tenon would have been fine, but the rear leg angle could have caused fitting problems. Dowels were a good alternative, but I found the pocket screw method to be the easiest and most accurate.

There are areas where two mortise-and-tenon joints intersect. It depends where you place the back assembly mortises. You can move the joints slightly toward the rear of the leg to avoid this situation, however, I prefer to trim one of the tenons during dry fitting.

Ash is a nice hardwood to work with for a project of this type. The boards for this chair had been air dried for a couple of years and did have some checks and cracks, but since I was gluing stock for the legs, I could choose the best outside surfaces.

Use exterior-rated fasteners and glues. I found the polyurethane glue to be an excellent choice for this project. It set up in a reasonably short time and the joints were solid.

Variations and Options

This style of bench is common in North America. The big, bulky, heavy-looking bench is quite different in appearance from the more delicately styled English garden bench.

To illustrate the differences in the two styles, I mocked up an arm and leg assembly common to the English style and photographed it beside the project bench.

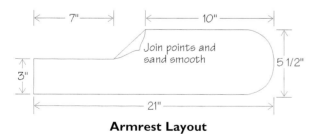

Armrest Layout

The choice is a matter of personal taste but both styles are popular.

It's possible to use almost any hardwood for this project. Teak and mahogany are often used in the high-end commercial models built by specialty companies. Companies specializing in garden furniture sell these benches at very high prices. A few companies have a complete line of chairs, benches and tables in this style.

The bench can be finished with any good outdoor stain. There are dozens of colors available, so picking one to suit your taste won't be difficult.

Enjoy this bench in a garden setting, on a deck or on a front porch. It will last for many years and provide hundreds of hours of peaceful relaxation.

English Garden Bench Variation

Using a Stop Block

Clamp a board on the line where the top surface of the arm meets the back leg. This will prevent the arm from creeping upward as you tighten the pocket screws.

CHAPTER 5

High-Class Octagon Patio Table

Many people have had the experience of running around looking for "another" table for the family barbecue. We always seem to be short that extra table for the punch bowl or extra space when a large crowd gathers. Well, look no more. This high-class octagon patio table will fill all your needs and then some.

As is the case with all of the projects in this book, I've built the table using a combination of materials and finishing. I hope it will give you alternative choices for your project, but almost any material and finishing combination can be used as long as you account for the environment. For example, if you plan to use this table in your Florida sunroom, just about any wood can be used. On the other hand, if this table is to be left outdoors in the rain and sun, you need to take a little more consideration of the wood and finish choices to maximize its life.

The table shown was built with select cedar. As with all select woods, it can be expensive. Given the conditions and intended use, this table can be made from just about any wood you have available. Construction-grade cedar, pine or even pressure-treated spruce will work, but make sure the moisture content of the wood is below 15 percent.

To add a little class to the table, Cetol 1 by Sikkens (number 045 mahogany protective translucent finish for exterior wood) was applied. The manufacturer suggests three coats applied at 24-hour intervals. For application techniques on new wood, refer to chapter two.

This project is an excellent example of various woodworking techniques and can be used to teach the young woodworker some of the basics. If you have a son or daughter who's been asking to help in the workshop, this is the ideal project.

Mortise-and-tenon joinery is used throughout this project. They can be cut by hand or with power tools depending on the equipment available and your experience. Biscuit or plate joinery is the technique of choice for attach-ing the table frame. Don't let the lack of a biscuit joiner stop you from building the table; dowels can be easily used in their place.

Notice that the cross supports are fitted to the legs with mortise-and-tenon joints (see "Octagon Table"). To distribute the weight and add a little extra strength, the corner table slats beside each cross support are secured tightly with rabbet joints tying the frame and supports to-gether.

The spacing between slats is kept to a minimum. Its only purpose is to allow water to easily run off the table in an outdoor situation. If the table is to be used exclusively in an enclosed sunroom or porch, you can reduce the spac-ing. It may require selective trimming to the width of the slats and a bit of trial and error, but it can be easily accom-plished. My table will spend a good portion of its life out-side, so I've used wider spaces to allow for water runoff.

For this project, I've decided to use an exterior con-struction glue that comes in a tube. All joints will be glued, particularly the rabbet-to-slat joints. Exterior-grade or "outdoor" screws have been used to secure the slats from the underside.

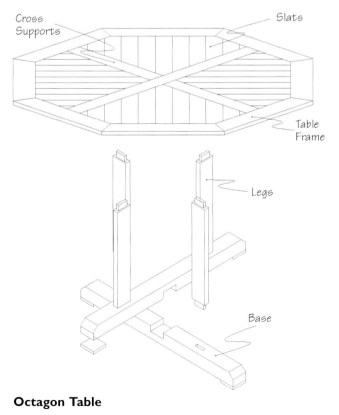

Octagon Table

Octagon Patio Table

Number	Part	Dimensions (Thickness × Width × Length)
2	Base	3½″ × 3½″ × 36″
4	Legs	1½″ × 3½″ × 27¼″
4	Feet	¾″ × 3½″ × 3½″
8	Top Frame	1½″ × 3½″ × 20″
2	Cross Supports	1½″ × 3½″ × 42⅞″

In order to get these parts, you will need to find or purchase the following lumber and supplies:

Number	Nominal Stock Size	To Yield These Parts
1	4″ × 4″ × 6′	Base
1	2″ × 4″ × 10′	Legs
2	2″ × 4″ × 8′	Table Frame
1	2″ × 4″ × 8′	Cross Supports
6	1″ × 3″ × 8′	Slats

You'll also need four small scraps of wood for the sacrifice pads and 2½″ and 1¼″ outdoor screws. Construction-grade exterior wood glue (any brand) is also required.

Construction Steps

1 Cut two 3½″ × 3½″ × 36″ boards for the base.

2 Layout the mortises and half-lap joints as shown in "Base Layout." Be certain that the half-lap dadoes are oriented correctly with respect to the mortises.

3 Cut the half-lap dadoes. I've used a table saw in this case, but a radial arm saw or handsaw and chisel will work equally well.

4 Cut 45° corners on each end of the base to soften the bulky appearance of the base. Test fit as shown.

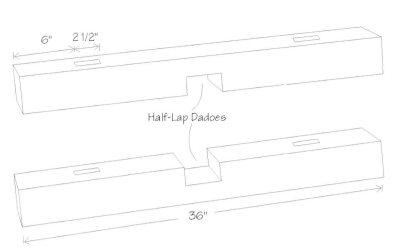

6″ 2 1/2″

Half-Lap Dadoes

36″

Base Layout

20″

2 3/4″

3/4″

22 1/2°

Table Frame Pieces

Step 2

Step 3

Step 4

Step 5

Step 8

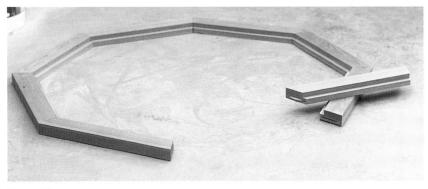

Step 11

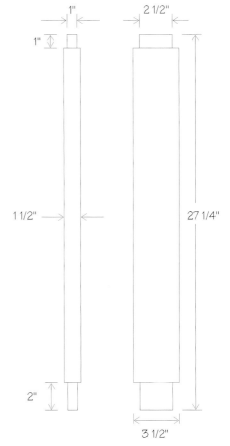

Leg Layout

5 Create the base assembly mortises 2″ deep by 2½″ long by 1″ wide to accept the leg tenons.

6 Create the four legs by cutting four 1½″ × 3½″ × 27¼″ long pieces from a 10′ length of 2 × 4 lumber (see "Leg Layout").

7 Using a table saw or router table, cut the leg's lower tenons at 1″ thick by 2½″ wide by 2″ high. The upper tenons are 1″ thick by 2½″ wide by 1″ high. Test fit the mortise-and-tenon joints as you create them to ensure the best possible fit.

8 Assemble the base as shown using exterior waterproof construction cement and four 3″ outdoor screws.

9 Make the table frame pieces using two 2″ × 4″ × 8′ boards. Prior to cutting the eight pieces to size, plough out a rabbet ¾″ × ¾″ with a table saw or router table. Creating the rabbet prior to cutting the angled table frame pieces will save time and form a better fit (see "Table Frame Pieces").

10 Test assemble the frame to ensure all pieces are cut correctly.

11 Biscuit or dowel joinery can be used to assemble the table frame.

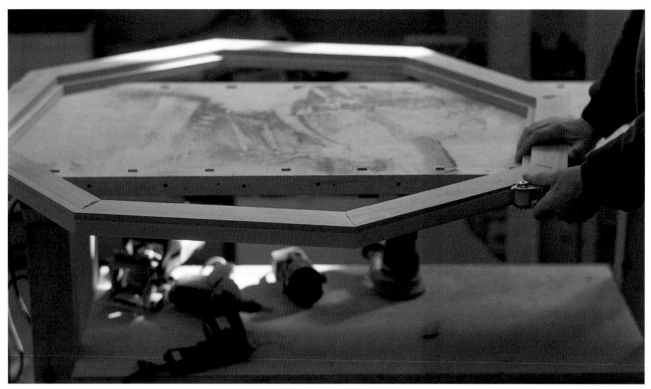

Step 12

12 Assemble the table frame with glue and secure with a band clamp for twenty-four hours. The band clamp will ensure tight joints as well as allow you to carefully install other parts on the frame.

13 Cut the two cross supports and form the rabbets, half-lap, and mortise joints as detailed in "Cross Support Layout." Attach to the table frame with glue and screws from the underside. Remember to predrill the screw holes to achieve maximum hold and avoid splitting the wood.

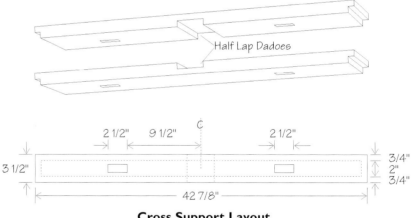

Half Lap Dadoes

Cross Support Layout

Step 13

14 The rabbet joint between the cross support and table frame should be as illustrated in the photo. Position each support at the center of its respective table frame member. This will guarantee equal sections for the slats.

15 Begin fitting the slats with the first slat in each section running from the cross support center to the table frame center. The simplest method to determine correct slat size is to mark an oversized piece in place, then cut to size.

16 Slat spacing is set at ⅛" and the last slat is a right triangle. It strengthens the cross support to table frame connection. Glue and screw each slat in place. Screws are installed from the underside and slightly countersunk.

Step 14

Step 15

Step 16

17 Install each slat by measuring an oversized piece in place and then cut accurately. The process is a little slow, but the appearance is heavily dependent on how the slats are installed.

18 Turn the table upside down and install the legs. Apply glue inside the mortise and "pin" the joint with a wood screw through the side. Install the base to the legs in the same manner. Draw the joint tightly together by inserting a screw into each tenon through the underside of the base.

19 Attach four small 3″ × 3″ sacrifice pads to the base. These pads help when placing the table on uneven ground and, more importantly, are the only contact with the damp earth or deck. They will be the first pieces to rot, so secure the pads with two screws. As they rot over the years, simply replace the pads.

20 Use a ¼″ roundover bit to ease all of the sharp corners on the base, legs and around the upper and lower outer edges of the table frame. It saves a bruise or cut if someone bumps the table and softens the overall look. The table is now ready for final sanding and finishing.

Step 17

Step 18

Step 20

Construction Notes

Don't skimp on the glue when building outdoor projects. A little squeezed out, if not in an area that affects the looks of the project, will only add protection.

Try and get the joints as close fitting as possible. Always use fasteners that are rated for outdoor applications. They cost a little extra but are well worth the expense.

When applying the finish, pay special attention to the area where two boards meet. Apply a little extra paint. If there is a possibility that the joint will trap water, provide drainage holes. Water, air and dirt trapped in a joint are the enemies of wooden furniture.

As I said earlier, this project is a great teaching aid for the novice woodworker. It highlights mathematical principles such as the eight 45° table frame joints forming a perfect 360° circle. A youngster that believes math serves no purpose in the real world will be intrigued by all the angles and triangles. It is also a great project to teach layout and the basics of mortise-and-tenon joinery.

Variations and Options

Almost any wood can be used to build this table. On a three-seasons porch, pine is an alternative. For the upscale setting, mahogany is unbeatable. If you need a table to hold planters in a garden setting, use pressure-treated lumber as an inexpensive and elegant option. This table lends itself to many applications.

Slat direction can be altered if you wish. Run them parallel to the table frame boards for a totally different look. However, make sure the first slat next to the table frame board is tight to the frame so water isn't trapped in the rabbet.

And finally, the choice of finishing options is endless. If the wood is beautiful with a lot of character, clear-coating is the answer. A couple of people who wandered into the shop during the building of this cedar table said they would definitely use a clear protectant on it.

The table can also be given a more delicate appearance by reducing the dimensions of the base. The legs can be turned for a more classical look and spread out or moved inward. The options are many and varied. Try to maintain adequate stability with your new design or alterations as well as the normal table height of 30″ if you want to use the table with standard chairs.

CHAPTER 6

A Potpourri of Planters

Raised Panel Planter

Plank Planter

Post-and-Panel Planter

I f you've just finished building your new deck or completed that long-planned siding project, don't throw away the scrap lumber! Planters are an ideal way to make use of the so-called "waste" wood that's often left over after finishing a large project. Or you may not have completed a project but have dozens of pieces of wood that you've saved because "someday they'll come in handy." Well, today is the day!

Many woodworkers enjoy building small garden planters because they add a touch of elegance to a garden bench or furniture grouping.

Our planters will detail three woodworking styles: raised panel, plank and post-and-panel construction.

The raised panel planter is constructed of birch and illustrates the technique of making raised panels on a table saw. This method is useful for many other projects including kitchen cabinetmaking, furniture and raised panels for wall coverings.

The plank planter is a straightforward, low-cost way to create movable backyard planters. It employs basic construction techniques and is a great way to put those short end pieces of wood to good use. This particular plank planter is made of ash; however, you can use any wood type. I just happened to have some short pieces of ash in

the shop, so they were rescued from the firewood bin.

And finally, there's a post-and-panel planter made from pine and stained a mahogany color. It's a great style addition to colonial or old English garden settings.

All of these planters have a "sacrificial" bottom board because it's usually the first part to rot. Dirt and moisture are in constant contact with the bottom board, even if the plant is in a container. Due to watering or rain, this board usually gets soaked. I've suggested that holes be drilled in the bottom to help the drainage, but that's only a delay tactic. This board will have to be changed every so often.

Don't nail or glue the bottom board to the planter frame. Leave it loose and use the cheapest piece of plywood available. You can often get construction-grade fir plywood at a reasonable price, and it makes a great bottom board.

Have fun building these planters. They're easy to construct, inexpensive and add much more than their worth to a deck or garden. These designs are also a great place to start teaching woodworking techniques to the youngster who's been wanting to help build a project. Everybody wins: The children finally get into the shop, the gardener gets a beautiful planter, and you get some quality shop time.

Construction Steps
RAISED PANEL PLANTER

1 Begin making the raised panel sections by cutting eight stiles (the frame's vertical member) at ¾″ × 1½″ × 19½″, and eight rails (the horizontal members) at ¾″ × 1½″ × 9½″.

2 Cut dadoes in the center of one edge on each stile and rail that's ⅜″ deep by ¼″ wide.

3 The center raised panel is made from four boards that are ¾″ × 10″ × 17″. The overall width and height of the panel is equal to the width and height on the inside of the stile-and-rail frame plus the depth of two dadoes. Therefore, the height of the panel is calculated by adding the inside frame height of 16½″ plus the two dado depths of ⅜″ for a total dimension of 17¼″ as illustrated in "Raised Panel Layout." The frame is ¼″ less than the actual dimension so that the panel will "float" to account for expansion and contraction of the wood. The ¼″ is subtracted from the overall width as well as the height.

4 The panels must be scored by cutting a ⅛″-deep groove, 2″ in from each edge on all four sides of the blank.

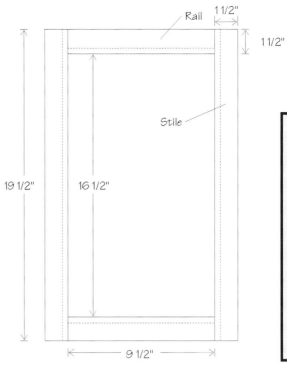

Raised Panel Layout

> ## Cutting Dadoes
> When plowing a dado on a table saw or router table, set the bit or blade as close as possible to cut in the center of the board. After the first pass, reverse the board and run it through a second time. This procedure will guarantee that the dado is perfectly centered.

Step 2

Step 4

Raised Panel Planter

Number	Part	Dimensions (Thickness × Width × Length)
8	Stiles	¾″ × 1½″ × 19½″
8	Rails	¾″ × 1½″ × 9½″
4	Panels	¾″ × 10¼″ × 17¼″
1	Plywood Bottom	¾″ × 11¾″ × 11¾″
4	Top Frame	¾″ × 1½″ × 13¼″

To get these parts, you will need to find or purchase the following lumber and supplies:

Number	Nominal Stock Size	To Yield These Parts
1	1″ × 12″ × 6′	Panels
3	1″ × 2″ × 8′	Stiles and Rails
	Scrap Plywood	Platform

5 To "raise" the panel, set the saw blade at 10° and slightly less than 2″ high. Test cut on a piece of scrap to determine that the taper is set correctly. The first ⅜″ of each taper should be no more than ¼″ thick, as detailed in "Panel Taper Detail," so the panel will move freely in the dado. You may have to alter the angle to achieve this dimension.

6 Next, cut a ¼″-wide by ⅜″-deep dado in the center of each rail so you can join the frame using a spline technique.

7 Cut and install ¼″-thick by ¾″-wide by 1″-long wood splines as shown in "Using Splines." This is only one of the many joinery techniques possible. I could have used biscuits, dowels or plug-filled holes for screws at each corner joint. The choice is yours.

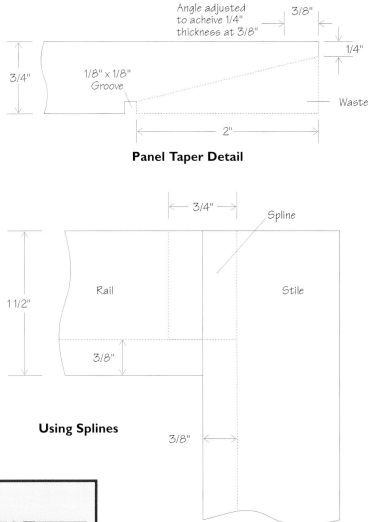

Panel Taper Detail

Using Splines

Raising Panels

Install a board on the table saw fence to assist you in cutting high panels and rail ends, as illustrated in the photograph.

Step 6

Step 7

8 Assemble all panels with the spline and glue. The joint can be pinned with a brad nail or left in clamps until the glue sets.

9 Attach the four panels to each other with screws and glue. Fill the holes with wood plugs. Do not use a screw that is too long. You may interfere with free panel movement and the expanding panel will crack the frame.

10 Cut four small angle blocks by sawing across the width of a 1″ × 4″ board at a 45° angle. Attach in place on the bottom of the planter as shown with glue and screws.

11 Any type of feet can be installed on the corner blocks. In my project, I used four ceramic doorknobs that I had around the shop. Cut small, angular feet or round wood balls, or buy one of the many commercial feet offered in your hardware store.

12 Install a ¾″-thick by 1½″-wide horizontal frame, mitered at 45°, around the perimeter on the top of the planter. This frame hides the spline joints and is a nice touch to finish the project.

13 As with all of our planters, a scrap piece of plywood, loosely fitted into the base supported by the corner blocks, will hold the plant container. Drill holes in the plywood for drainage.

Step 9

Step 10

Step 11

Countering Wood Movement

Do not glue panels in the frame. They must be free-floating to allow for expansion and contraction.

Construction Steps

PLANK PLANTER

1 Build a pressure-treated frame using 2″ × 2″ stock. The dressed size of these boards is 1½″ × 1½″ square. They are readily available at any lumber store. You'll need four stretchers at 21″ long, four uprights at 9″ long, and four rails at 12″ long. The frame should measure 12″ wide by 12″ high by 24″ long.

2 Attach each corner with exterior construction adhesive and 3″-long exterior screws.

3 Cut two pieces of the same stock at 1½″ by 1½″ by 24″ long and attach as shown. These boards will support the scrap plywood platform that will hold the pots. The position of these boards will be determined by the type of plant. Use 3″ treated screws, but don't apply glue to the joints. If the plant style is changed, the platform support boards can be raised or lowered. Cut and install a plywood platform.

> ### *Dry Fitting Parts*
>
> Prior to gluing the joints, dry fit all parts. Before final assembly, clear-coat the wood with a preservative in potential trouble areas, such as the grooves of the stiles and the rails of the raised panels.

Plank Planter

Number	Part	Dimensions (Thickness × Width × Length)
4	Stiles	1½″ × 1½″ × 9″
4	Rails	1½″ × 1½″ × 12″
4	Stretchers	1½″ × 1½″ × 21″
2	Bottom Supports	1½″ × 1½″ × 24″
1	Plywood Bottom	¾″ × 9″ × 21″
8	End Planks	¾″ × 3″ × 12″
16	Side Planks	¾″ × 3 3/16″ × 12″
2	Skirt Ends	¾″ × 3½″ × 13½″
2	Skirt Sides	¾″ × 3½″ × 25½″
2	Cap Ends	¾″ × 1½″ × 12″
2	Cap Sides	¾″ × 1½″ × 24″

To get these parts, you will need to find or purchase the following lumber and supplies:

Number	Nominal Stock Size	To Yield These Parts
3	2″ × 2″ × 8′	PT Frame
5	1″ × 4″ × 8′	Panels, Skirt, Cap
	Scrap Plywood	Platform

Step 1

Step 3

4 The panel boards you choose will determine the layout. However, for the ash panels, I attached four boards per end at ¾″ thick by 3″ wide by 12″ long. Each side had eight boards ¾″ thick by 3³⁄₁₆″ wide by 12″ long. The side length increased by 1½″ because of the added thickness of the two end panel boards. Apply construction adhesive and fix each panel in place with 1½″ galvanized nails at the top and bottom.

5 Add a lower skirt using 1½″-wide boards that are mitered at the corners. Prior to installing the lower skirt, round over the upper outside face with a ¼″ roundover bit. The same style of skirt is installed on the top, but the lower outside face is rounded over. To complete the planter, install a cap frame of ¾″-thick by 3½″-wide boards that are mitered on the corners to match the upper and lower skirt. Round over the cap's outside surface as well as the inside of the frame. Sand and finish as desired.

Step 4

Step 5

Construction Steps

POST-AND-PANEL PLANTER

1 Prepare four posts, cut from an 8' length of 3″×3″, at 2¼″×2¼″×20″ long.

2 Mark and cut mortises as shown in "Post Detail."

3 Using the table saw, cut a kerf ⅛″ deep around the outside of the top on each leg.

4 A 45° cut is made to all four sides on the top of each post, ½″ down from the top.

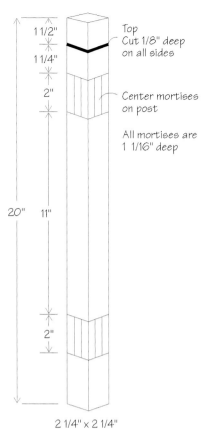

Top
Cut 1/8″ deep
on all sides

Center mortises
on post

All mortises are
1 1/16″ deep

1 1/2″
1 1/4″
2″
20″ 11″
2″

2 1/4″ × 2 1/4″

Post Detail

Step 2

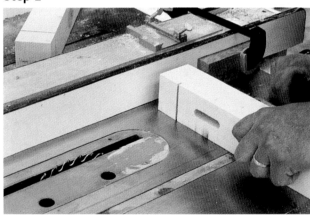

Step 3

Step 4

Avoiding Splits

Predrill a pilot hole when screwing together 2 × 2 boards. This wood tends to split easily, and the pilot holes will provide a better grip for the screw and help avoid splitting.

Post-and-Panel Planter

Number	Part	Dimensions (Thickness × Width × Length)
4	Posts	2¼″×2¼″×20″
8	Rails	1½″×2½″×16″
16	Panel Pieces	¾″×3½″×11″
4	Bottom Supports	¾″×1½″×12″
1	Plywood Bottom	¾″×15¾″×15¾″

To get these parts, you will need to find or purchase the following lumber and supplies:

Number	Nominal Stock Size	To Yield These Parts
1	3″×3″×8′	Posts
2	2″×4″×8′	Rails
2	1″×4″×8′	Panels
	Scrap Plywood	Platform

5 Prepare eight rails with a finished size of 1½″ thick by 2½″ high by 16″ long. Form the tenons on each end. (See "Rail Detail.")

6 Cut a ¾″-wide by ¼″-deep dado in the center of one 1½″ edge on each of the rails.

7 Each of the four sections formed when connecting the posts and rails will require four panels at ¾″ thick by 3½″ wide by 11″ long.

8 Attach an upper and lower rail to a post with the rail dadoes facing each other. Slide in four of the panels.

9 Apply glue to the rail tenons and attach another post. Continue in the same manner until the four post-and-panel sections are assembled. Clamp all the posts and set aside until the glue dries.

10 Cut and attach four platform support boards with screws and glue. These board measurements are not critical, but we made each ¾″ thick by 1½″ wide by 12″ long.

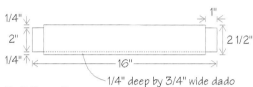

1/4″ 2″ 1/4″ 1″ 2 1/2″ 16″

1/4″ deep by 3/4″ wide dado

Rail Detail

Avoiding Kickback
Don't use the table saw fence in combination with the miter gauge, as this can cause the stock to bind and kick back. Clamp an offset board in front of the blade to set distances as shown in the photograph.

Step 5

Step 8

Step 9

Step 10

11 Cut a scrap piece of plywood with drainage holes and lay it on the support boards.

12 Give the planter a final sanding and it's ready for finishing.

Step 11

Step 12

Construction Notes

These planters will be subjected to the wind, rain and sun, and they will be in some form of contact with soil that is watered and fertilized to feed the plant. For these reasons, be careful about joint failure, cracks in the wood and areas that can collect moisture. Take a close look at the potential problem areas. Is there a place that will hold moisture? If so, apply exterior caulk or drill drainage holes.

Give these planters an extra coat of stain or paint as an added measure of protection. Clean them from time to time and inspect areas that seem to be deteriorating. To protect the floating panel dado on the raised panel planter, apply exterior silicone to the joint. This caulk will allow the wood to move but will not let water enter the joint.

Variations and Options

Planters are enjoyable to build because the only design limitation is your imagination. I've seen some innovative ideas around town.

Just about any wood is suitable. If the planters are going to be painted a solid color, investigate your options of using inexpensive, pressure-treated lumber. Scrap lumber is also ideal for these projects.

The raised panel planter can be any height or width desired. This is true for all of the planters in this chapter.

If you decide to use paint on the panels, give them a coat before assembly. This will prevent seeing a paint line when the panels contract. You can also achieve some dramatic effects by painting the panels a different color.

Raised panel planters can have the panel assemblies turned sideways for a low, wide planter. You can use a 45° miter joint where the panels meet in place of a butt joint.

The plank planter can be 2′ or 20′ long. It is also ideal as a seat support. Build two and string 2 × 4s between them for a great deck seat.

The post-and-panel planter is another style that can be used to create a deck bench. Again, build two and attach 2 × 4s to the tops of the rails.

The legs on the post-and-panel planter can be extended 6″ or 8″ below the bottom rail to create a different look. The panels don't have to be butt joined, they can be tongue-and-groove boards with a bead detail.

These three styles can be designed in many lengths, widths and heights. There is guaranteed to be one that is ideal for your family plant enthusiast.

CHAPTER 7

Garden Wishing Well

When I began the research for the projects in this book, I hadn't considered a wishing well. However, a few friends said they'd really like to have a unique plan for a garden well. During the next month, I began to notice how many people had wishing wells in front of their houses. I hadn't paid attention before, but now that a well was on my potential project list, I began to notice dozens of designs.

I then decided to include a plan for a well, but I wasn't impressed by the examples I had seen. Most were innovative, but I wanted something that really looked like an old-time well!

I looked through some old books at the library and noticed certain similarities of style with these wells. They all had a wooden base and uprights of some type to support a small roof. I'm not sure what original purpose the roof served, but it was a beautiful detail.

Cedar and pine seemed to be the wood of choice. Most old farms had the wells painted with a milk paint or none at all, which resulted in a weathered gray structure. All had a wooden bucket with a tired-looking rope to pull the water from the well.

It was obvious that I had to scale down the old farm full-size well structure. I decided to try a few mock ups in the shop and came up with the design for the well detailed in this chapter. It's about 6′ tall and a little

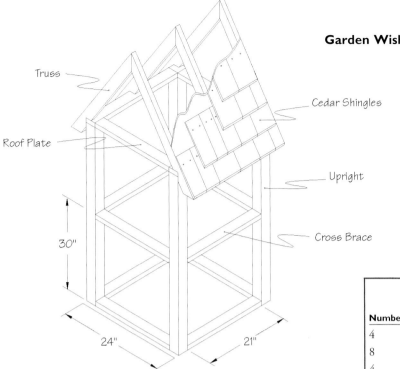

Garden Wishing Well

Truss

Cedar Shingles

Roof Plate

Upright

Cross Brace

30"

24"   21"

over 2′ square. Just right for the average garden or front lawn!

I've used construction-grade western cedar with 4″ tongue-and-groove vertical siding to reflect old-time bead board. Many wells weren't this fancy, but a few were very detailed—obviously built by a proud craftsperson.

The roof is covered with hand-split cedar shingles. This feature was common in areas where cedar was cheap and plentiful. The rope is a piece of frayed line that I meant to throw in the garbage many times.

The bucket is simply ¾″-thick cedar boards, cut at an angle to form a "round" bucket. This type of pail was very common and often made by the owner/farmer. A few examples I saw were much better constructed with metal bands, which meant the town was lucky enough to have its own cooper.

The popularity of this project really surprised me. During construction of the well, the majority of shop visitors wanted one. Comments such as "My parents had one in their yard and I've always wanted one" were common. I now have about six more to make and only about a dozen people have seen the finished project.

This is an enjoyable project to build, but be warned—you'll end up making more than one. In fact, you may just spend half the winter making wishing wells. Which, come to think of it, isn't a bad way to spend the winter months.

Garden Wishing Well		
Number	Part	Dimensions (Thickness × Width × Length)
4	Uprights	1½″ × 1½″ × 60″
8	Cross Braces	1½″ × 1½″ × 21″
4	Roof Plates	1½″ × 1½″ × 21″
28	Siding Boards	¾″ × 3½″ × 29¾″
4	Wide Corner Boards	¾″ × 2½″ × 30″
4	Narrow Corner Boards	¾″ × 1¾″ × 30″
8	Face Boards	¾″ × 2½″ × 21½″
4	Ledge Boards	1½″ × 5½″ × 28″
6	Common Rafters	1½″ × 3½″ × 20″
2	Fascia	¾″ × 3½″ × 24″
10	Sheathing	¾″ × 3½″ × 24″
3	Gable Siding	¾″ × 3½″ × 8′
2	Bucket Support	¾″ × 3½″ × 24″
1	Handle	1″ × 5″ Dowel
1	Shaft	1″ × 27″ Dowel
1	Connector	¾″ × 1½″ × 5″
8	Bucket Pieces	¾″ × 3⅛″ × 10″
1	Bucket Bottom	¾″ × 1″ × 8″
½	Bundle	Cedar Roof Shingles

To get these parts, you will need to find or purchase the following lumber and supplies:

Number	Nominal Stock Size	To Yield These Parts
6	2″ × 2″ × 8′	Frame
11	1″ × 4″ × 8′	T&G Siding and Gable End Panels
4	1″ × 3″ × 8′	Face Boards
1	2″ × 6″ × 10″	Ledge
4	1″ × 4″ × 8′	Roof Sheath, Bucket, Crank Assembly
2	2″ × 4″ × 8′	Rafters
1	1″ × 36″ Dowel	Handle and Crank
½	Bundle	Cedar Roof Shingles

Construction Steps

1 The frame will be built with 2 × 2 cedar lumber that is readily available from your local lumberyard. Or you can rip 2 × 4 stock to size. Prepare four boards that are 60″ long and 1½″ square.

2 Sand the four uprights and ease all of the edges with a router equipped with a ¼″ round-over bit.

3 Cut eight cross braces at 1½″ × 1½″ × 21″ long.

4 To build the well framework, attach two of the cross braces to two uprights as shown in "Garden Wishing Well" on page 55. Then connect the two frames to each other as shown in the photo.

5 Cut and attach four boards at 1½″ × 1½″ × 21″ to the top section of the frame that will form the roof plates.

6 To ensure the frame is square and stays square, we'll need four corner blocks. These are simply right triangles cut from a 1 × 4 piece of lumber at 45°.

7 Install one block at each corner with construction adhesive and screws in predrilled holes as shown.

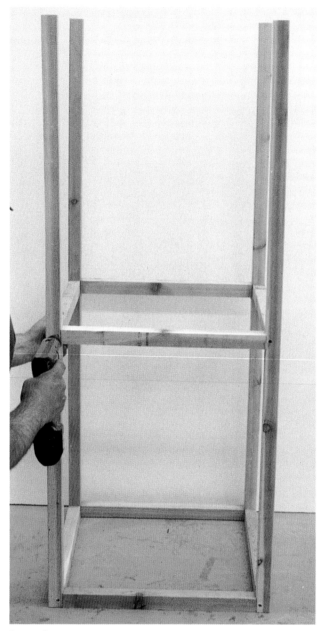

Step 4

Step 5

Step 7

Step 8   **Step 9**   **Step 10**

8 Install 28 siding boards at ¾″ × 3½″ × 29¾″ with a bead of construction adhesive and 1½″ galvanized common nails at the bottom and top of each board. Cover all sides. I have used tongue-and-groove boards that were less than 3½″ wide. However, any type of siding can be used for the well. Don't be overly concerned about the corners as they will be covered. Hold the boards flush with the top of the middle brace, which will raise them slightly off the ground.

9 Each corner will be faced with two boards. You'll need four at ¾″ thick by 2½″ wide by 30″ long and four at ¾″ thick by 1¾″ wide by 30″ long.

10 Cut and attach four upper and four lower face boards at ¾″ thick by 2½″ wide by 21½″ long. However, verify the measurement prior to cutting the boards since it will vary depending on the thickness of the siding boards used. Run a bead of construction adhesive from corner board to corner board and attach the face boards with two small finishing nails. The adhesive will secure the boards once it cures.

Step 11

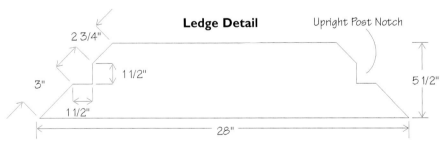

Ledge Detail

Upright Post Notch

2 3/4″

1 1/2″

3″

1 1/2″

5 1/2″

28″

11 The well ledge is made from 2 × 6 stock, mitered at each corner and notched to fit around the uprights. Each well is slightly different, so custom fit the ledge boards one at a time. However, the starting layout is detailed in "Ledge

Detail," which I used for the project well. Once the boards are dry fit and you're satisfied, apply a bead of adhesive and secure the boards with a 2½″ screw from the underside of the cross brace.

Rafter Assembly

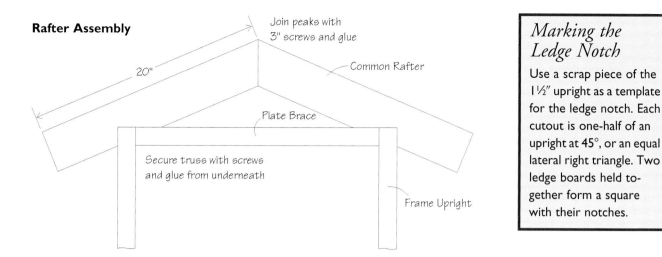

Join peaks with
3" screws and glue

Common Rafter

20"

Plate Brace

Secure truss with screws
and glue from underneath

Frame Upright

Marking the Ledge Notch

Use a scrap piece of the 1½" upright as a template for the ledge notch. Each cutout is one-half of an upright at 45°, or an equal lateral right triangle. Two ledge boards held together form a square with their notches.

12 Building roofs and calculating rafter dimensions are intimidating to many people. However, there are simple mathematical formulas that can be applied to find common rafter sizes. I'll detail these principles in chapter thirteen on building gazebos, but for now follow the drawing in "Rafter Layout." Six common rafters are needed to begin framing the roof. The angle at the peak is cut at 22½° and matched at the bird's mouth notch to hold the rafter angle plumb at its peak. Assemble the rafters with glue and a 3″ screw holding the peaks together as shown in "Rafter Assembly." Install the rafters with one set flush at the front uprights and one set flush with the back uprights. Center the third set. Using construction adhesive and one 3″ screw per joint, secure the rafters at the top plate from the underside as shown.

13 Unlike sheathing for an asphalt shingle roof, cedar shingle roofs are covered with boards that are spaced to allow air circulation under the shingles. The spacing is equal to the amount of exposure or distance between the shingles, referred to as the *reveal*. Since we will

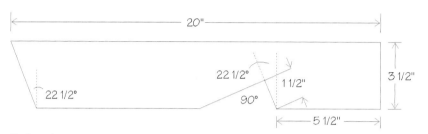

20"

22 1/2°

22 1/2°

1 1/2"

90°

3 1/2"

5 1/2"

Rafter Layout

Step 12

use a 4½″ reveal when installing the cedar shingles, the "on-center" spacing of the roof boards is 4½″. Cut twelve boards at ¾″ thick by 3½″ wide by 24″ long. Two will be used as fascia boards covering the ends of the rafter tails, and the remaining ten will be used to sheath the roof.

Fascia boards are attached with construction adhesive and nails. One board covers the end of the rafter tails, on each side. The first roof board is attached flush with the outside edge of the fascia board and all of the other boards are placed to the peak at 4½″ on center.

14 The same tongue-and-groove siding that was attached vertically on the base was used to cover both gable ends of the well. The number and length of boards is dependent on the slope of the roof or directly related to the rafter length. In this case, I used four lengths of siding that were cut shorter as I progressed higher on each gable end. As shown in the photo, mark each board in place to accurately determine the correct length and angle. Start at the bottom of each gable end, clamp the board in place and mark and cut to size. The first or lowest board is held flush with the bottom of the rafter tail. Attach the siding boards with construction adhesive and a finishing nail.

15 Once the gable ends are covered, the roof can be shingled. The first row is a double row. Set the first row on each side so the shingles overhang the fascia board by 1″ and the gable ends by ⅜″. The second row is placed on top of the first row, covering the joints. Begin the second row 4½″ up from the edge of the first row. Use two ¾″ galvanized roofing nails per shingle, each 1″ from the edge and 5½″ from the bottom of the shingle as shown in "Shingle Layout."

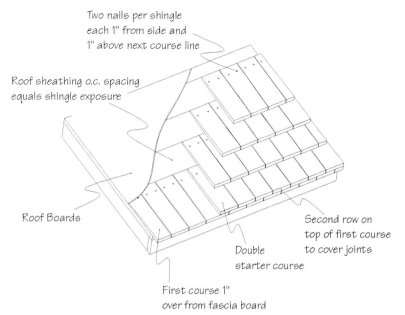

Two nails per shingle each 1" from side and 1" above next course line

Roof sheathing o.c. spacing equals shingle exposure

Roof Boards

Second row on top of first course to cover joints

Double starter course

First course 1" over from fascia board

Shingle Layout

Step 13

Step 14

Step 15

16 The ridge cap is a series of cedar shingles that were all cut 4″ wide. The exposure is 4½″ and each row is alternately overlapped as shown.

17 To begin the assembly of the decorative water bucket, cut and shape two boards as shown in "Support Arm Layout." Note that one support arm has the 1″ hole drilled completely through the board, while the other hole is drilled ½″ deep. Attach each arm to the uprights 12″ above the well ledge boards with adhesive and a 2″ screw per side.

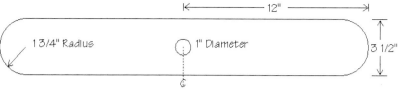

Support Arm Layout

Step 16

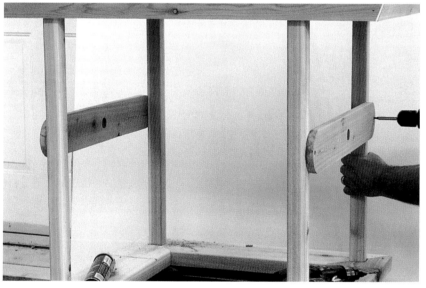

Step 17

Shingle Spacing

We're not concerned about building codes with our wishing well, so just about any shingle exposure is acceptable. You might prefer to use a 3″ reveal or a wider 6″ reveal to save on shingles. The choice is yours. On center roof board spacing should roughly match the shingle reveal. But always start sheathing the roof by placing the first board flush with the outside surface of the fascia board, and work toward the roof peak.

Avoiding Splits

Use 3″ exterior-rated screws to join the framework, and predrill the screw holes to minimize splitting the wood.

18 Build the bucket crank assembly using two 1"-diameter dowel rods cut at 27" long and 5" long and a connector board as shown. The connector board is ¾" thick by 1½" wide by 5" long and all edges are eased with a ¼" roundover bit.

19 Attach the handle assembly to the well by placing the 27" dowel through the hole in one support arm and butted against the bottom of the hole in the other arm. Hold the assembly in place with a ¼" by 1"-long lag bolt. Drilling a pilot hole slightly smaller than the bolt's shaft diameter is necessary to prevent splitting the dowel rod. Place a washer on the bolt and attach securely.

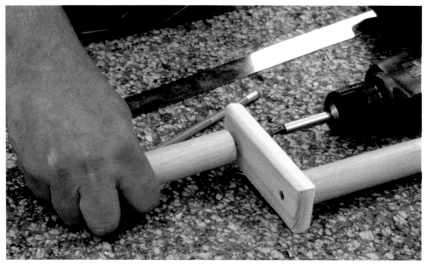

Step 18

Step 19

Step 20

Step 22

20 The water bucket is made up of eight boards from 1 × 4 stock. They are 3⅛″ wide by 10″ long and cut at a 22½° angle on each side. When joined with biscuits and glue, the bucket is made up of eight 45° angles equaling a 360° circle.

21 Once the glue sets, lay the bucket on a 1 × 8 piece of ¾″ stock and trace the bottom from the bucket's inside. Cut and install with glue and brad nails.

22 Locate an old rope and wind it on the crank assembly. Drill two holes opposite each other in the bucket's side near the top, and thread the rope. The wishing well is now ready for final sanding and finishing.

> ### *Masking Tape Clamps*
> Use two biscuits per joint. Or, if you haven't got access to a biscuit cutter, use dowels or splines. This is a "rustic" water bucket for our well, so the joints aren't critical—in fact, the rougher the better. You can use simple glue joints and masking tape to hold the bucket staves together until the glue sets.

Construction Notes

Building the well is a fairly straightforward, simple process. The only area that might be a little intimidating is the roof construction and cedar shingle application.

Those of you who haven't ever built a roof can use this project to begin learning how to do roof framing. The cedar shingle application is a little more difficult because it's such a small roof. I used standard shingles, but you may want to use the smaller shakes to lessen the rapid buildup as you lay each course.

Information about cedar shingle and shake installation is available on the Internet at the Cedar Shake and Shingle Bureau Web site (http://www.cedarbureau.org). They provide diagrams and information brochures about their products and proper installation techniques.

Cedar is a relatively soft wood and tends to split very easily. It's advisable to drill pilot holes for all of the fasteners. Nailing close to the end of a board can also cause splitting, so drilling a small pilot hole or blunting the nail point is helpful.

The project well will be left unfinished, which means it will turn gray over time. It also means that wood deterioration may occur sooner if the bottom is in contact with the earth. You might consider a clear protectant if the well will be placed in a damp area.

Variations and Options

One obvious variation is the choice of wood. Cedar may not be common in your area and pine may have been the wood of choice for the old wells. You can use any wood that's readily available, even old barn boards for that authentic, old-time appearance.

I'm really pleased with the scale of the well, but you may find it a little large for a small garden setting. If that's the case, build one at half scale.

Another option is the choice of roof shingle. There are many available, including asphalt, tile or metal. Quite a few that I came across opted for the asphalt shingle. If you plan on using one of these options, sheath the roof with ½″ plywood.

You may decide to paint your wishing well a color that matches other structures in the garden. If so, you can use pressure-treated wood that is easily painted with a good exterior solid finish. If you plan on using cedar or redwood and want to preserve the natural tones, finish the well with a clear preservative.

And finally, as with all outdoor furniture projects, investigate the potential problems of wood deterioration. Is the well in close contact with soil? Will it be subjected to wind and rain? If the conditions are going to be severe, take some extra precautions to protect the wood. The outdoor conditions should always be an important factor when deciding on wood and finishing products.

CHAPTER 8

Deck Serving Cart

The idea for this project came to me when I was helping a friend barbecue hamburgers and hot dogs for the little league baseball team he coached. We had all the food cooking and nothing but two little wood side tables, attached to the barbecue, on which to place our food, sauce and utensils. It was quite a balancing act and a couple of hot dogs fell to the ground. We were a little annoyed, but the family dog thought it was quite acceptable—he had two hot dogs for lunch.

It was obvious that a serving cart, much like those fancy tea wagons some folks have in their dining rooms, would be ideal. However, it would be used outside, so it had to be ready to take a fair amount of abuse from the weather. I also had to design the cart with large enough wheels that would easily roll across many different surfaces.

The design I finally arrived at seems to be working just fine. It's a great place to put food while someone is cooking and handy for wheeling the prepared food to the table. The cart has a lower table for extra carrying capability. A condiment rack was built on the top tray to hold bottles of sauces and relishes needed at the barbecue and table. The rack holds quite a few bottles and doubles as a portable bar for deck parties.

Once again I dug into my pile of rejected ash and birch to build the serving cart. Since most of this project would be built of 1½″-wide material, I could easily salvage all the boards from less than perfect planks.

I decided to stain the cart with Sikkens Cetol 1 #014 Driftwood exterior stain, which would even out the color of the wood. I applied three coats to the cart and was careful to add a little extra stain to the areas where water would collect.

The serving cart is constructed using very simple butt joints. The majority of joints are secured with glue and screws. You don't need any special tools to build the cart with the exception of a lathe to turn the wheels. However, with a little care and patience, the wheels could be cut using a jigsaw.

This is one of those great weekend projects that will become a useful addition for those outdoor parties. It doesn't cost a lot to build and makes a great gift for someone who has everything.

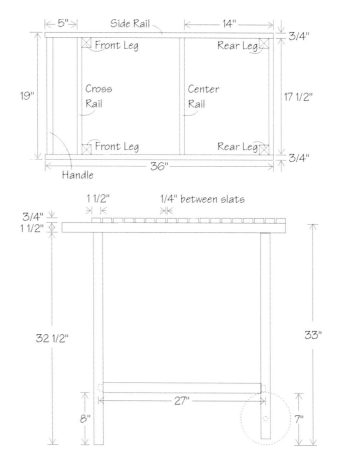

Deck Serving Cart

Number	Part	Dimensions (Thickness × Width × Length)
2	Top Side Rails	¾″ × 1½″ × 36″
1	Handle	1″ × 18″ Dowel
3	Top Cross Rails	¾″ × 1½″ × 17¹⁄₂″
2	Rear Legs	1½″ × 1½″ × 33″
2	Front Legs	1½″ × 1½″ × 34″
2	Bottom Cross Rails	¾″ × 1½″ × 14⁵⁄₈″
2	Wheels	¾″ × 8″ Diameter
18	Top Shelf Slats	¾″ × 1½″ × 20½″
16	Bottom Shelf Slats	¾″ × 1½″ × 17½″
4	Condiment Rack Stiles	¾″ × 1½″ × 6″
2	Condiment Rack Rails	¾″ × 1½″ × 5″
2	Condiment Rack Stretcher	¾″ × 1½″ × 19″

To get these parts, you will need to find or purchase the following lumber and supplies:

Number	Nominal Stock Size	To Yield These Parts
13	1″ × 2″ × 8′	Frame, Slats
1	2″ × 2″ × 12′	Legs
1	1″ × 18″ Dowel	Handle
1	⅝″ × 20″ Dowel	Axle
1	1″ × 8″ × 24″	Wheels

Construction Steps

1 Cut two main side rails ¾″ thick by 1½″ wide by 36″ long.

2 Slightly round over one end of each rail with a belt sander.

3 Locate a point ¾″ from the edge and ¾″ back from the rounded end of the side rail. Drill a 1″-diameter hole in each side rail, ¼″ deep.

4 Cut an 18″ piece of 1″ dowel rod. Inset the rod into the rail holes and drill a pilot hole using the spade bit exit marks as a guide. Counterbore the pilot hole, insert the screws and plug the holes. Sand the wood plugs flush when the glue dries.

5 Cut two ¾″ × 1½″ × 17½″ cross rails and attach them to the side rails. Glue and screw the assembly, making sure to counterbore the screw holes so they can be filled with a plug.

6 Sand all wood plugs flush and final sand the rail assembly. Round over the outer surfaces of the assembly, top and bottom, with a ¼″ roundover bit or by hand with sandpaper.

7 Cut two front legs at 1½″ square by 34″ long, and two rear legs at 1½″ square by 33″ long. Note the different leg lengths and their position on the frame assembly. These are cut to specific lengths to accommodate the cart's wheels. Now is an ideal time to round over and sand smooth all of the edges of the legs.

Step 3

Step 4

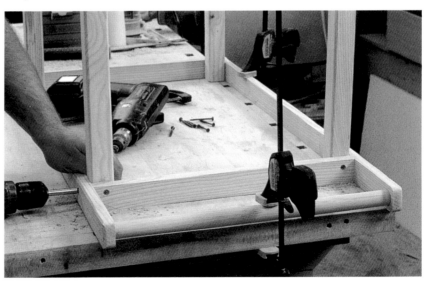

Step 8

8 Attach the two 34″ legs inside the front cross rail and the two 33″ legs inside the rear cross rail. Use a 1½″ screw, glue and wood plug to secure the legs. Install two screws per leg, one through the side rail and the other through the cross rail into the leg. Slightly stagger the screws on the rails so they won't hit each other when driven into the leg.

9 At this point, install an additional cross rail, ¾″ × 1½″ × 17½″, midway between the two end rails. This center rail will help keep the side rails parallel to each other.

10 Two lower side rails, ¾″ × 1½″ × 27″, should now be installed on the inside of the front and back legs to support the lower platform. These two rails are set back ¾″ from the outside edge of each front and rear leg. They are 7″ up from the bottom of the rear legs and 8″ up from the bottom of the front legs.

11 The ¾″ lower rail set back will allow us to install the lower rear cross rails between the cart legs. Cut two rails at ¾″ × 1½″ × 14⅝″ and install as indicated in the photo.

12 Turn two ¾″-thick by 8″-diameter wheels on the lathe or alternately cut them with a jigsaw.

Marking the Center

Use a 1″ spade bit to drill the hole. The bit's point will slightly exit the other side of the rail when you reach the ¼″ depth, and this mark becomes the center mark of the hole.

Step 10

Step 11

Step 12

13 Drill a ⅝″-diameter hole in the center of each wheel. Block the rear legs of the cart with a 1″-thick spacer so the cart is level on the workbench. Place the wheel in position and mark the legs, then drill a ⅝″ hole in the center of each rear leg.

14 Enlarge the holes in the rear legs with a wood rasp so that a piece of ⅝″-diameter by 19¼″-long dowel will turn freely. This dowel rod will act as an axle for the wheels.

15 Apply polyurethane glue to the holes in the wheels and press them onto each end of the dowel rod. The moisture-cured polyurethane glue will expand and lock the wheels securely to the dowel.

16 The top shelf slats are ¾″ thick by 1½″ wide by 20½″ long. Prepare 15 pieces at this size; sand and round over the top surface with a ¼″ roundover bit. Three additional pieces are needed to complete the top shelf. They are cut at ¾″ thick by 1½″ wide by 19″ long so we can install the condiment rack. Install the slats with a ¼″ space between them starting with a ¼″ overhang on the front cross rail. The 15 slats at 20½″ overhang the side rails equally on both sides and the 19″ rails are installed flush with the outside surface of the side rails. Use 1½″ screws to secure the slats, one per side. Counterbore the holes and install tapered wood plugs.

17 The bottom shelf slats are installed in the same manner. Cut 14 boards at ¾″ thick by 1½″ wide by 17½″ long. Two additional slats at 14⅝″ long are installed between the legs as the first and last board for the shelf. The spacing is approximately ¼″, but I suggest you lay all of the boards in place and verify your spacing before securing them to the bottom rail.

> ## *Aligning the Holes*
> Use a ⅝″ spade bit to easily mark the center of the hole on the rear legs. The flanges of the bit, through the hole in the wheel, will force the drill bit's point to center.

Step 13

Step 15

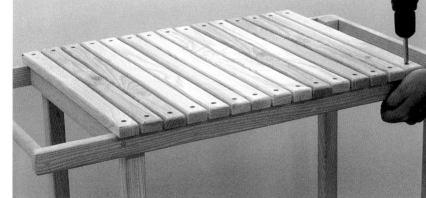

Step 16

18 Plug all screw holes and sand them flush.

19 The condiment rack is simply four pieces of ¾″-thick by 1½″-wide by 6″ long stock. They are installed vertically as shown in the photo, two per side.

Step 19

20 The horizontal frame, supported by the four vertical boards, consists of two boards ¾″ by 1½″ by 19″ long and two shorter boards at ¾″ by ½½″ by 5″ long. Assemble, round over the inside and outside surfaces and attach as shown. The deck serving cart is complete and ready to be stained.

Step 20

Construction Notes

One area that needs special attention is the width of the shelf slats. If they are cut wider or narrower than 1½″, you will not be able to space the slats at ¼″. A ⅟₆₄″ increase in slat width will add up over 18 boards.

It's not a critical issue and you can use any width slat as long as you dry fit the boards before securing them in place. Even if you're sure the slat width is 1½″, it would be wise to dry fit. I had a little problem with the project cart for that very reason. So, as my father always said, "Do as I say, not as I do." He didn't want me to see his mistakes either!

Another key area that should be addressed is the process of hole counterboring. Invest a little money in a carbide-tipped drill and counterbore bit. It will cut clean, perfectly round holes in the slats, allowing you to tightly fit the plugs. After sanding, they'll be very hard to see and it looks professional.

Take your time enlarging the holes for the wheel axle. If possible, use a fine rasp and gently file the hole so it remains round but opens up a little to allow the rod to spin freely. If you have a 16mm metric drill bit, try a test hole in a scrap piece of lumber as this bit is slightly larger than ⅝″.

Variations and Options

This cart can also be used as a potting cart for the gardener. You might want to consider larger diameter wheels if the terrain is rough. The rear legs can be shortened by 1″, and 12″ wheels can be installed.

The cart can be equipped with wheels stocked by most home centers. The axle for those models is a bolt that can be attached to the rear legs.

You may have a special application for this all-purpose cart that requires wider boards. The slat width can easily change to any dimension without causing any major changes to the cart's frame.

A heavy-duty model can be built. Increase the side and cross rail widths to 3½″ and you'll dramatically increase the load capacity of the cart.

This deck serving cart can be built out of any wood species you prefer: cedar to match existing furniture, or pressure-treated lumber that will be painted. If you plan on using this cart as a barbecue accessory, change the side board slats on your barbecue to match the cart.

This is another project I enjoyed building. It isn't complicated and goes together in a weekend. It's a fun project for the youngsters and a unique accessory for your deck that will impress the neighbors. They won't be able to run to the home center and buy one.

Comfortable Garden Swing

Do you realize how many people want a freestanding garden swing? I didn't, but I soon found out when friends and customers visited my shop. The response to this project was unbelievable!

The first person that saw the swing bought it. Apparently it's a very popular item. I think I'll start specializing in garden swings. Forget the cabinetmaking. From now on it's full steam ahead with swings!

One thing I did discover when researching this swing project was the need for a freestanding unit. We often see a swing hanging from the perfect tree in movies, but most of us don't have a strong tree in our yard that has the necessary thick branch running parallel to the ground.

Therefore, in my mind, the swing would have to be freestanding, easily taken apart for winter storage, light enough to be moved by a couple of strong people and, above all else, comfortable. After looking at many designs and then trying a few in the shop, I decided on this project swing. It has all of the important features and looks good. The frame is strong, the chair moves freely and it's comfortable to sit in even when the chair is not moving.

The swing is made out of construction-grade cedar. The wood is marked S-GRN, meaning the tree was cut into boards shortly after harvesting. The wood is wet, so expect a certain amount of shrinkage. Construction-grade cedar is the least expensive building material to use unless you have a wood lot or opt for painting pressure-treated wood.

If you do decide to use cedar, look around for a lumberyard that allows customers to pick through the wood. Some lumber stores in my area are self-serve, and I suspect there's one or two in most areas. You may pay a few cents more, but the ability to sort the wood is worth the price.

After building this project, I checked out some of the commercial swings for sale in my area. Most were selling at double the materials cost for this swing, and the quality left a lot to be desired. Although it's a fairly expensive proposition to build this project, there's a lot of value for your time and money.

Don't cut corners on material or hardware. Buy the best wood you can afford and use only exterior-rated galvanized and stainless steel fasteners.

I was told the chain I purchased is plated for outdoor use, but I'm a little suspicious. Time will tell. I believe there is a plastic-coated version of this chain, which may be a more suitable option. It might be worthwhile to do a little research. The chain could also be replaced with a plastic-coated or stainless cable.

This was one of the most comfortable chairs I've used. I say *was* because the swing is gone! Now I have to start building another one for my place, and this time I'll hang onto it. Good luck with your swing. I know you'll enjoy every minute relaxing with a nice cool drink.

Garden Swing

Number	Part	Dimensions (Thickness × Width × Length)
4	Frame Legs	3½″ × 3½″ × 96″
1	Cross Beam	3½″ × 3½″ × 72″
2	Upper Cross Braces	1½″ × 5½″ × 22¾″
4	Lower Cross Braces	1½″ × 3½″ × 72″
2	Angle Cross Braces	1½″ × 3″ × 18″
2	Front Seat Supports	3″ × 3″ × 14″
2	Rear Seat Supports	3″ × 3″ × 22″
2	Seat Rails	1½″ × 3½″ × 18″
3	Seat Stretchers	1½″ × 3½″ × 47¾″
12	Back Rest Slats	¾″ × 3½″ × 23⅞″
5	Seat Slats	1½″ × 3½″ × 50¾″
2	Arms	1½″ × 3½″ × 25″

To get these parts, you will need to find or purchase the following lumber and supplies:

Number	Nominal Stock Size	To Yield These Parts
6	4″ × 4″ × 8′	Legs, Beam, Chair Supports
2	2″ × 4″ × 12′	Lower Cross Braces
1	2″ × 6″ × 4′	Upper Cross Braces
7	2″ × 4″ × 8′	Seat Rails, Angle Braces, Stretchers, Seat Boards, Arms
3	1″ × 4″ × 8′	Backboards

Hardware: Chain, Bolts, Screws

Construction Steps

BUILDING THE SUPPORT FRAME

1 Mark each of the four 3½″ × 3½″ × 96″ beams that will become the frame legs as shown in "Leg Layout." Notice that the angles on the top and bottom are 22½° and the notch depth is 1¾″, or half the beam's thickness.

2 Cut both 22½° angles on each leg with a circular saw.

3 Then complete the cuts on each leg with a band saw or jigsaw. Sand the legs and round over with a ½″ roundover bit in a router.

4 Cut a cross beam measuring 3½″ × 3½″ × 72″ long. Sand and round over the edges.

5 Bolt the legs to the beam with a 6″ carriage bolt that's secured with a washer, lock washer and nut. Use exterior-rated hardware and drill a 1″ counterbore hole for the bolt head and another for the washers and nut assembly.

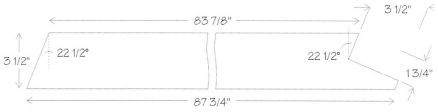

Leg Layout

Step 1

Step 2

Step 5

Cutting Safely

When using a circular saw to cut beams, particularly with angle cuts, use a square or other straightedge to safely and accurately guide the saw.

6 Clamp or attach temporary boards to hold the legs at 72″ wide as detailed in "Frame Layout." Clamp a 2 × 6 in place at the point where the upper cross brace is to be installed, and then level. Mark a reference line for the cross brace's upper edge. Verify that the measurement of the cross brace is as indicated in "Frame Layout." The overall width of the upper cross brace isn't critical and you can mark your cutting lines on the board. Verify that the dimension is close to that given for the cross brace in "Frame Layout."

7 Cut the upper cross braces to size, round over the outside faces and install with glue and three 3″ screws per side.

8 Install four lower cross braces, two per side. Attach with polyurethane glue and 3″ screws.

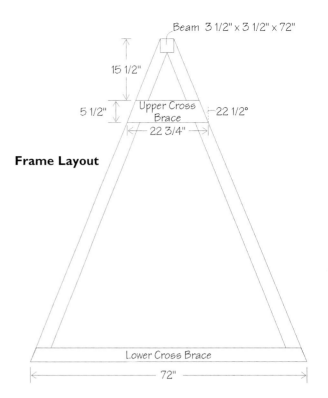

Beam 3 1/2″ x 3 1/2″ x 72″

15 1/2″

5 1/2″ — Upper Cross Brace — 22 1/2°

22 3/4″

Frame Layout

Lower Cross Brace

72″

Step 6

Step 7

Step 8

Using the Right Glue
Use polyurethane glue if the swing is being built with construction-grade cedar or other "green" wood. This is an ideal application for moisture-cured glue.

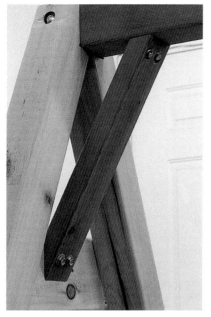

Step 10

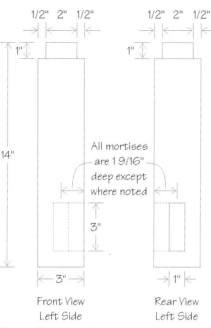
Angle Brace Detail

3"
30°   60°
18"

1/2" 2" 1/2"   1/2" 2" 1/2"
1"   1"
14"

All mortises
are 1 9/16"
deep except
where noted

3"

3"   1"

Front View   Rear View
Left Side   Left Side

Front Support Layout

Cutting Accurate Angles
Use the miter gauge on the table saw, set at 30° from a square cut, to cut the 120° angle on the angle braces.

9 At this point, make sure the beam is level, both leg assemblies are plumb and the inside leg-to-leg spacing is equal top and bottom, back and front.

10 Prepare two angle braces. The 120° end attaches to the cross brace. Secure the brace to the beam with two ⅜″ × 3½″ lag bolts and to the cross brace with two ⅜″ × 2″ lag bolts and washers. Be sure to drill pilot holes to avoid splitting the brace. Do not glue these braces in place if you plan to take the frame apart for storage. (See "Angle Brace Detail.")

BUILDING THE SWING SEAT

11 The front "legs," if this were a chair that touched the ground, are called front supports and the rear "legs" are labeled rear supports. Two front supports are required; cut to size and form the mortises as shown. (See "Front Support Layout.")

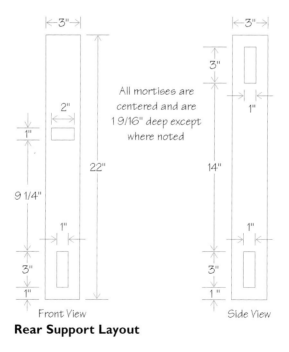

3"   3"
3"
2"
All mortises are
centered and are
1 9/16" deep except
where noted
1"
1"
22"   14"
9 1/4"
1"   1"
3"   3"
1"   1"

Front View   Side View

Rear Support Layout

12 Next, make the two rear supports. Use the completed front supports as a reference when marking the rear supports to avoid layout errors. (See "Rear Support Layout.")

13 Sand and round over all surfaces of the front and rear supports with a ¼″ roundover bit. Round over the top and bottom of the rear supports and the bottom of the front supports.

14 Cut two seat rails from boards 1½″ thick by 3½″ wide by 18″ long. The rails have a curved center section and an angled tenon to fit the rear support, which is best cut with the miter gauge on the table saw. Refer to "Seat Rail Layout."

15 Dry fit the front supports to the rear supports to verify that all of the joints are tight. Adjust tenons with a wood rasp if necessary to achieve a good fit.

Step 12

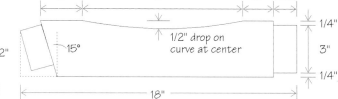

Seat Rail Layout

2″   11″   2″   1 1/2″

1/4″

1/2″ drop on curve at center

3″

15°

Trim waste to form 1 1/2″ deep tenon

1/4″

18″

Step 14

Temporary Curve Jig

Form the curve on the seat rail by creating the required bend in a thin piece of wood with a small clamp. Use this temporary jig to mark the curve line.

Step 15

16 Unlike a normal chair, this swing seat will be in motion, causing added stress to the joints. The mortise-and-tenon joints can be further strengthened using polyurethane glue and "pinning" with 2½" wood screws as shown.

17 Cut three seat stretcher boards at 1½" thick by 3½" wide with an overall length of 47¾". These three boards will support the seat and back boards. The front stretcher rail, as well as the lower rear stretcher rail, are joined to the chair supports at the intersection of the seat rail mortise-and-tenon joints. That joint reduces the mortise depth for the lower stretcher rails. Trim the stretcher rail tenons to fit, but maintain the tenon shoulder-to-tenon shoulder dimension of 44¾" on the stretcher rail. Apply polyurethane glue and pin the joints for added strength.

18 The back rest is made up of twelve boards ¾" thick by 3½" wide by 23⅞" long that are spaced ⅛" apart. Glue and screw the backboards to the upper and lower stretcher boards. Counterbore the screw holes and fill with wood plugs. Set the swing set on a flat surface and lay a 2 × 4 on the bench in front of the lower stretcher rail. Rest the back boards on this spacer board and secure them in place.

Step 16

Avoiding Clamping Damage

Long pipe clamps are often needed to hold joints until the glue sets. This is the case when securing the stretcher rails for the swing seat. A pipe clamp requires a couple of wood blocks to prevent damage to the project, and managing the clamp and blocks is very difficult. I've solved this problem by drilling holes in two pieces of wood and slipping them over the pipe. They're always ready and easy to handle when I need them.

Step 18

19 There are five seat slats required. One is 1½″ thick by 3½″ wide by 44¾″ long. The remaining four are 1¹⁄₂″ thick by 3½″ wide by 50¾″ long. Install the shortest seat slat at the front, between the supports and flush with the back edge of the front seat supports. The other four seat boards are installed ⅛″ apart. Secure the front board with four evenly spaced 2½″ screws into the front stretcher; the four other boards are fastened with one screw at each end. Use polyurethane glue and counterbored screw holes so they can be filled with wood plugs.

20 A thin piece of wood can be used to form a curved pattern on the back seat rails. Bend the wood to the desired curve, clamp in place and mark the curve. Verify that the highest point in the arc is centered on the chair and it starts from the same height on each end. Cut the back boards with a jigsaw and sand smooth.

21 Now is a good time to sand the seat and back boards before the chair arms are installed.

22 The arms are cut from two boards, each 1½″ thick by 3½″ wide by 25″ long as detailed in "Arm Layout." Use the table saw and miter gauge to rough out the tenon and file to size with a wood rasp.

Step 19

Step 20

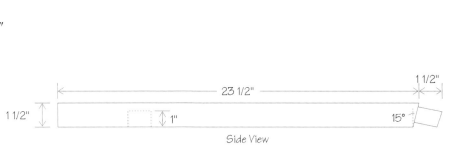

23 1/2″   1 1/2″

1 1/2″   1″   15°

Side View

Arm Layout

3 1/2″   1 3/4″ Radius   3/4″ 2″ 3/4″

25″

Top View

23 Once the mortise-and-tenon joint at the back of the arm is correct, lay the arm in place and mark the front mortise. Use the front support tenon as a guide.

24 Form the mortise on the underside of the chair arms and test fit. Once the fit is acceptable, cut the curve on the front of the arm. Sand the arms smooth and round over all edges except the end that joins the rear support. Apply polyurethane glue and clamp the arms in place.

25 Block the swing chair inside the frame, equal distances on both sides and the seat surface 16″ off the floor. Check that the frame beam and chair are level.

26 Drill a ⅜″-diameter hole in the outside center of the front support, 8″ up from the bottom. Use a level to locate the holes on the same plane for the back supports and drill ⅜″ holes in the back supports. Countersink the inside of both front support holes to recess the eye bolts. Install two ⅜″ × 2″ eye bolts in the front supports and two ⅜″ × 4″ eye bolts in the rear supports. Tighten in place.

27 The eye bolts will have to be opened enough to attach the chain.

28 Drill and install two ⅜″ × 4″ eye bolts through the beam at a width equal to the distance between the eye bolt centers on the chair. Mine measured 54″.

Step 23

Step 24

Step 26

29 Cut four equal lengths of chain and attach to the chair and beam. I used 1½″ link chain that had a 500-pound support strength rating. Each of the four pieces was 56″ long.

30 Test the chair making sure that it sits level and is at a comfortable height. It should swing freely inside the frame.

31 Clean all the joints of excess glue, give the swing a final sanding and it's ready to be finished.

Step 29

Construction Notes

Plan your cut list before you start cutting to minimize waste, particularly with the 2 × 4 material. The seat rails, stretcher boards, seat slats, angle braces and arms can be cut from seven 2 × 4s.

Glue and pin all mortise-and-tenon joints for maximum strength. The chair will be in motion and movement stresses the joints.

The most difficult joints to fit are probably the angled tenons from the arms and seat rails to the rear support. They can be completed successfully by cutting the tenon oversized and shaping with a wood rasp for a tight fit. It takes a little time and patience, but it's worth the effort. Getting a good, strong joint in these areas is important.

Buy the eye bolt and chain hardware at the same time. That way you'll be able to test how easily the chain slips onto the bolts. If it takes a little bit of twisting and pushing to get the chain over the eye, the fit is correct. Having a chain that comes off too easily is not a safe situation.

As I've said, the chair joints will be stressed due to movement, so use polyurethane glue, pin the joints and give the adhesive time to cure properly. It's necessary that you get the strongest joint possible.

Inspect the hardware on a regular basis to ensure all of it is correctly and securely attached. Look for weak joints as well as any abnormal wear.

The only potential problem area I've seen with this project is the angle braces. They will be subjected to a great deal of stress in many directions and could possibly fail. I'll monitor those joints over time and if they seem to be failing, I plan to have stainless steel braces made to replace those two boards. They appear to be working out just fine after a couple of months use, but it's worth inspecting the braces on a regular basis.

Variations and Options

The project swing was finished with three coats of Sikkens Cetol 1 #78 Natural stain, however, any high-quality outdoor finish is acceptable. Sikkens and other suppliers have translucent stains in a wide range of colors.

I used construction-grade cedar for this project, but any wood is suitable, particularly one of the hardwoods if you have an available supply.

The swing can be built to any size within the safe load-carrying capacity of the beam. However, extending the width another foot or two without changing the beam size should be fine.

The swing was designed to come apart for easy storage. Those of us who live in colder climates go through the storage and assembly rituals a couple of times each year. If you don't have to store the swing, all of the temporary connections can be made permanent with glue and additional hardware.

CHAPTER 10

Trellis Variations

Wall Trellis

Planter Box Trellis

I'm not an expert gardener, but I'm lucky enough to have friends and family who know a lot about the subject. I wanted to find out which trellis features would be desirable for the vine enthusiast. There were many answers, but one theme seemed to be common. Most gardeners wanted a trellis that was portable. It seems that many vines don't grow or survive outdoors in the harsh northern climates. Therefore, a trellis containing a growing vine that could be moved in and out of doors as the seasons changed was of great interest to my gardening friends.

With that theme in mind, I designed four trellises. The first is a simple wall trellis, the second is a planter box trellis, the third is a corner design and the fourth is a trellis with a wire grid. The boxes to contain the earth, as well as the trellis grids, are different in each style.

I also learned that the grid requirements for different species of vines are very specific. It apparently has a great

Corner Trellis

Wire Trellis

deal to do with the holding mechanics of the various vines.

You can mix and match the boxes and grid designs to meet the requirements of any plant. Additionally, the box may have to be enlarged to contain enough soil for the intended vine.

All of the trellis projects were finished with Sikkens translucent stain. I was extra careful when applying the stain and gave the interior of the boxes an additional application.

These trellises will take a lot of abuse simply because they are in direct contact with the earth. Be certain that there's adequate drainage and all of the joints are glued and fastened securely. The boxes will also be physically stressed by the soil and water pushing out from the inside.

The trellises are fun weekend projects that allow you some shop time and provides the family gardener with a gorgeous accessory. They're quick, simple and inexpensive to build, and none have any fancy joints.

The wall trellis is the only one without a soil box. It's designed to be driven into the ground near a wall or to be a freestanding unit in the garden. My planter box design has a grid that's angled. It's perfect for all kinds of flowering vines.

I was told by the woman whose garden you see in all of the project shots that the box for the corner trellis could be a little deeper given the area of trellis above the box. That's a point to keep in mind when you're building this project. Decide on the vine to be used and check out its needs in terms of soil volume and depth. If you need more volume, add another layer of 2×8 boards to the base.

And finally, the wire trellis was a hit with many gardeners. Most agreed that it was a perfect combination of grid size and box volume. This project visited the garden to be photographed and never left. My gardener friend said it was perfect for a plant that would winter indoors and enjoy the sun outdoors in the warmer months. It never came back to my shop, but it's got a great home now.

Construction Steps

SIMPLE WALL TRELLIS

1 Using two boards 1½″ thick by 3½″ wide by 96″ long, cut the following pieces: two at 1½″ × 1½″ × 72″, one at 1½″ × 1½″ × 60″, four at ¾″ × 1½″ × 22″, and four pieces for the center frame at ¾″ × 1½″ × 14″, which all have 45° cuts on each end.

2 Assemble the boards as shown in "Wall Trellis." Sharpen the lower ends of the two outside main boards so that the trellis can be driven into the ground. Assemble the parts using construction adhesive and 2″ exterior screws.

3 Sand and finish as desired. Apply a heavy coat of stain to the bottom of the trellis, which will be driven into the ground.

	Simple Wall Trellis	
Number	**Part**	**Dimensions** (Thickness × Width × Length)
2	Legs	1½″ × 1½″ × 72″
1	Center Upright	1½″ × 1½″ × 60″
4	Crosspieces	¾″ × 1½″ × 22″
4	Square Frame	¾″ × 1½″ × 14″

To get these parts, you will need to find or purchase the following lumber and supplies:

Number	Nominal Stock Size	To Yield These Parts
2	2″ × 4″ × 8′	All Pieces

Wall Trellis Layout

Construction Steps

PLANTER BOX TRELLIS

1 Cut 1 × 4 stock to the size and quantities shown in the materials list.

2 Build three sections using two 24"-long boards and two equal-sized side boards per section as detailed in "Planter Box Trellis Layout." Note the front panel is held flush with the top of the side panel. Install with construction adhesive and exterior-grade screws. The photo shows the box panels being assembled upside down to use the bench as a flat plane holding the boards flush at the top.

3 Stack the boxes, placing the smallest box on the bottom. Temporarily clamp together. Glue and nail two ¼"-thick by 1½"-wide by 22½"-long strips of wood over the front openings between the box sections.

Front Board   Back Board

Note: Install front board flush with top of side board

Angled Side Board

Box Section Detail

Planter Box Trellis Layout

Step 2

Step 3

Planter Box Trellis

Number	Part	Dimensions (Thickness × Width × Length)
6	Front and Back Boards	¾" × 3½" × 24"
2	Top Sides	¾" × 3½" × 12"
2	Middle Sides	¾" × 3½" × 10⅝"
2	Bottom Sides	¾" × 3½" × 9⅛"
4	Feet	¾" × 3½" × 3½"
2	Uprights	1½" × 1½" × 54"
1	Cross Brace	¾" × 3½" × 24"
4	Plant Supports	¾" × ¾" × 48"
1	Plywood Bottom	¾" × 7⅞" × 22½"

To get these parts, you will need to find or purchase the following lumber and supplies:

Number	Nominal Stock Size	To Yield These Parts
4	1" × 4" × '8	Box Panels, Upper Cross Board, Trellis Grid, Feet
1	2" × 2" × 10'	Uprights
	Scrap Plywood	Bottom Board

4 Attach four 3½″-square by ¾″-thick blocks to the bottom corners of the box. These will act as feet and support the planter base board.

5 Attach two uprights that are 1½″ square and 54″ long to each outside back corner of the box. Use glue and three screws per side, one through each back panel into the upright. The uprights are held flush with the bottom.

6 Cut a ¾″-thick by 3½″-wide by 24″ board and attach flush with the top of the uprights. This cross brace is installed on the front face of the uprights.

7 Secure four ¾″-square by 48″-long boards from the box to the upper cross brace. These boards can be arranged in any pattern. I've angled mine in a fan arrangement as shown.

8 Cut a scrap piece of plywood to act as a throwaway base inside the box. Drill holes for drainage. Sand and apply an exterior finish to the trellis.

Construction Steps
CORNER TRELLIS

1 Cut the base boards from 2 × 8 stock. Use either a radial arm saw or table saw to form the angles on the ends of all boards.

2 Assemble the boards as shown in "Corner Trellis Layout." Use construction adhesive and 3″ exterior screws.

3 Two boards from 2 × 4 stock are cut and attached to the base. They will raise the trellis off the ground and support the scrap plywood base board. The pieces are

Step 4

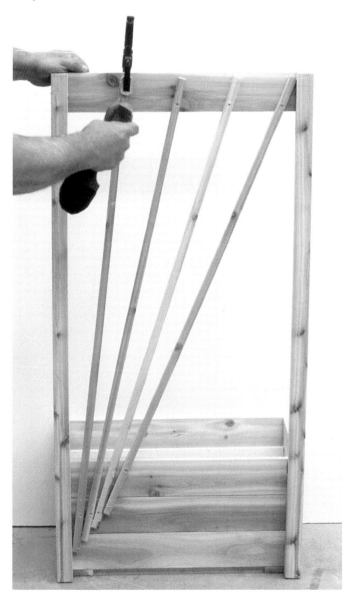

Step 7

installed as indicated in the photo. After attaching the boards with adhesive and 3″ screws, sand and round over the bottom surface with a ¼″ roundover bit in a router.

4 The 33¾″-long foot is set back 1½″ from the front face of the trellis box. The short 13¼″ foot is 3″ in front of the back corner.

5 The four trellis uprights are ¾″ × 1½″ × by 72″. Attach one per corner with screws and glue, making sure the bottoms are flush with the bottom of the trellis box.

6 Secure the top of the uprights with two horizontal braces. Cut one ¾″ × 1½″ × 24″ and the other at 23¼″ long. Attach them flush with the top of the uprights.

7 You can cut any number of crosspieces to form the trellis grid. I used 20 boards at ¾″ × 1½″ × 24⅝″. The ends of each crosspiece were cut at a 10° angle. Install the boards from top to bottom on one side and bottom to top on the other. The angled ends were installed flush with the outside upright.

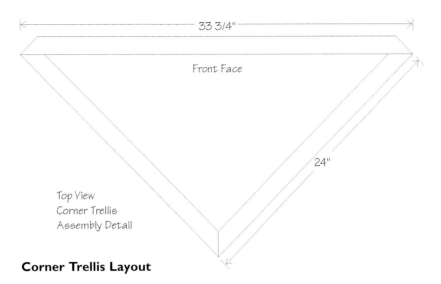

Top View
Corner Trellis
Assembly Detail

33 3/4″

Front Face

24″

Corner Trellis Layout

Step 1

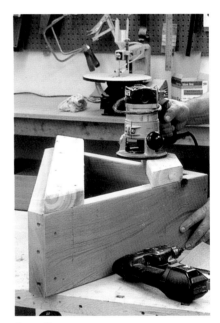

Step 3

Step 5

Corner Trellis

Number	Part	Dimensions (Thickness × Width × Length)
2	Base Sides	1½″ × 7½″ × 24″
1	Base Front	1½″ × 7½″ × 33¾″
1	Front Foot	1½″ × 3½″ × 33¾″
1	Rear Foot	1½″ × 3½″ × 13¼″
4	Uprights	¾″ × 1½″ × 72″
2	Cross Braces	¾″ × 1½″ × 24″
20	Grid Pieces	¾″ × 1½″ × 24⅝″

To get these parts, you will need to find or purchase the following lumber and supplies:

Number	Nominal Stock Size	To Yield These Parts
1	2″ × 8″ × 8′	Base
1	2″ × 4″ × 48″	Feet
1	1″ × 4″ × 12′	Uprights
5	1″ × 2″ × 10′	Grid Boards

Construction Steps

WIRE TRELLIS

1 Build four 2 × 2 frames and four 2 × 4 frames.

2 Shape the upper and lower outside edges of all frames using a ½″ roundover bit in a router.

3 The frames are stacked, beginning with a 2 × 2 frame as the bottom layer, and secured using a bead of construction adhesive and 3″ exterior-rated screws.

4 Prepare the two uprights at 1½″ × 3½″ × 60″ long. A ¼″-wide by ½″-deep dado is then cut into one 3½″ face of each board.

5 Drill a series of ³⁄₁₆″ holes through the uprights in the middle of the dadoes for the vine wire. I spaced the holes 6″ apart starting 6″ from the top; the last hole is 18″ from the bottom.

6 Attach the uprights inside the trellis box. Check that the box is sitting level in both directions and plumb the uprights in the center of the short sides. The dadoes should be facing to the outside on both boards.

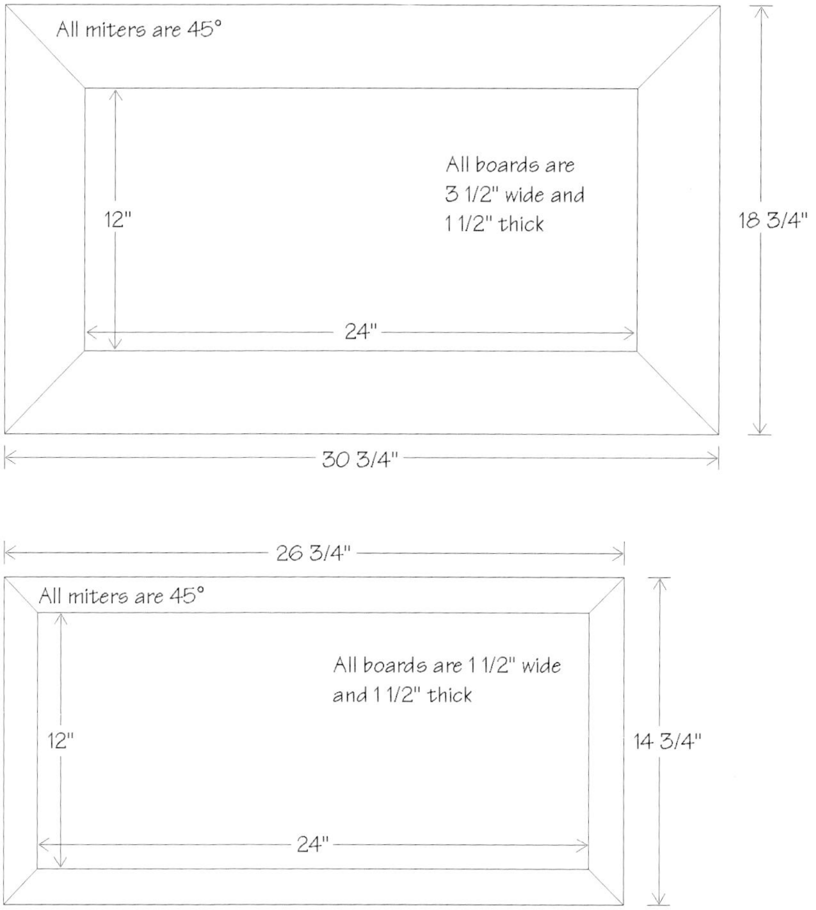

All miters are 45°

12"

All boards are 3 1/2" wide and 1 1/2" thick

18 3/4"

24"

30 3/4"

26 3/4"

All miters are 45°

12"

All boards are 1 1/2" wide and 1 1/2" thick

14 3/4"

24"

Wire Trellis— 2 × 4 and 2 × 2 Frames

Wire Trellis

Number	Part	Dimensions (Thickness × Width × Length)
8	2 × 4 Frame End	1½″ × 3½″ × 18¾″
8	2 × 4 Frame Side	1½″ × 3½″ × 30¾″
8	2 × 2 Frame End	1½″ × 1½″ × 14¾″
8	2 × 2 Frame Side	1½″ × 1½″ × 26¾″
2	Uprights	1½″ × 1½″ × 60″
1	Top Support	1½″ × 3½″ × 30¾″
2	Bottom Supports	1½″ × 1½″ × 22″
1	Plywood Bottom	¾″ × 12″ × 24″

To get these parts, you will need to find or purchase the following lumber and supplies:

Number	Nominal Stock Size	To Yield These Parts
6	2″ × 4″ × 8′	All Pieces
	Scrap Plywood	Base

Step 8

7 Cut a top support that's 1½″ thick by 3½″ wide by 30¾″ long. Cut a radius curve on each end and round over the board, top and bottom, with a ½″ roundover bit. Install the support as shown with construction adhesive and screws. Check that the spacing between uprights is equal at the top and bottom. The top support should also overhang the uprights equally on each side.

8 You'll need about 20′ of plastic-coated wire to thread the trellis grid. Start threading a continuous run from top to bottom. At the start of the run, loop the wire around a roundheaded screw and anchor the wire. The screw can be driven into a counterbore hole so it's below the upright's surface. Pull the wire tight and anchor the other end in the same fashion.

9 If your saw blade is thin enough, you will have a narrow strip of wood leftover after cutting the 1½″ square frame pieces from the 2 × 4 stock. Cut two of these strips at ¼″ thick by 1½″ wide by 47½″ long. Attach them to the uprights so each dado is covered.

10 Install two platform support boards that are 1½″ square and 22″ long in the bottom of the trellis box. These two boards will support the scrap plywood base. You'll have to notch the plywood platform to fit around the uprights. The trellis is now completed after a final sanding and a few coats of stain.

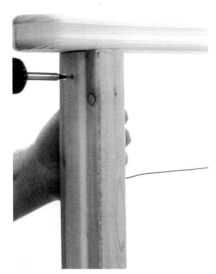

Step 9

Construction Notes

I've used exterior construction adhesive available in a caulking tube for most of the projects in this chapter. It seems to work well in securing and sealing the joints, and it's relatively inexpensive.

I didn't try to get a perfectly smooth surface on these trellises. The rough surface contrasts with the delicate flowers in a rustic look that many people enjoy.

These trellises will most likely be outside, so don't skimp on the wood preservatives or stain, and the trellises will last as long as possible.

Try to anticipate where water will collect and provide drainage holes. The loose plywood platforms will have to be changed from time to time. There is a pressure-treated plywood available as well as a marine-grade plywood that is constructed with waterproof glue.

Screws will always hold better and longer than nails. Where possible, use screws to secure all connections. If the screw heads are exposed to the weather, counterbore and plug the holes. With the wire trellis project, use plastic-coated or exterior-rated grid wire.

Variations and Options

There is one question to ask when designing and building planters and trellises: What are the requirements of the plant that will be grown in this container?

According to my gardening friends, vines have special needs in terms of container size, grid pattern and trellis material. Some need rough, porous surfaces while others can climb on just about any surface.

All of the project trellises can be modified in terms of container size, grid material and dimension. You might want to use a wire grid on the planter box trellis or a chicken wire style of grid on the wire trellis. The choice is yours and the options are endless.

Just about any wood will make a great trellis. If the intent is to paint the wood, use inexpensive, pressure-treated lumber. If you want something fancy indoors, use one of the beautiful hardwoods.

CHAPTER 11

Adirondack Furniture Ensemble

I'm fortunate to live near one of the most beautiful areas in the world. The Thousand Islands, as this vacation spot is called, lies on the U.S. and Canadian border, between New York State and the Province of Ontario. It has hundreds of miles of waterways, well over a thousand islands and scenery that takes your breath away.

In the early nineteen hundreds, the Thousand Islands was the vacation playground for the rich and famous. Hotel owners, movie stars and politicians gathered to enjoy all the pleasures this place had to offer.

There are stately "summer" homes on the islands, including three or four castles that I've seen. There's a story that one of the famous hotel owners in New York City had his summer home chef create a new salad dressing for a special dinner party at his "cottage." That dressing is

known as Thousand Islands Dressing. Quite a salad dressing and quite a "cottage," which is as big as four normal-size homes.

This resort seems to have more garden furniture jammed into a few hundred square miles than anywhere in the world. One of the most common styles you'll see is the Adirondack chair and settee. There are hundreds of examples.

Given all the research material that was available, I headed to the area. I looked at dozens of styles and variations on the Adirondack furniture theme. Between those examples, a few plans friends had and a bit of testing in the shop, I built this version of the famous Adirondack furniture. To accompany the chair and settee, I've added a simple coffee table. The three pieces create an ideal setting and are very comfortable.

There aren't any complicated joinery techniques. Adirondack furniture uses straightforward glue-and-screw joints. A good jigsaw, sander, drill and screw gun are all the tools you'll need. In fact, you could build this furniture with simple hand tools.

Many people feel building Adirondack-style furniture is complicated. However, just the opposite is true: It's a simple woodworking project. The heart of the design is the rear leg. Once it is laid out and cut, the difficult part is behind you.

The ensemble is made of ash with a couple of pieces of birch that were in my wood bin, which are great hardwoods for these types of projects. The stain on the project set is Sikkens Cetol 1 #014 Driftwood.

I'll detail the chair construction and then explain some of the differences when building the settee. The coffee table is also straightforward with easy-to-assemble butt joints.

If you're thinking about spending a lazy afternoon with a cool glass of lemonade and a good book, this chair will meet your needs. It's comfortable, has good-sized arms to hold a glass and is a great place to take a nap if reading gets a little tiring.

Take your time building this set and make sure all of the joints are well secured because these pieces will be popular and well-used additions to your outdoor furniture.

Construction Steps
ADIRONDACK CHAIR

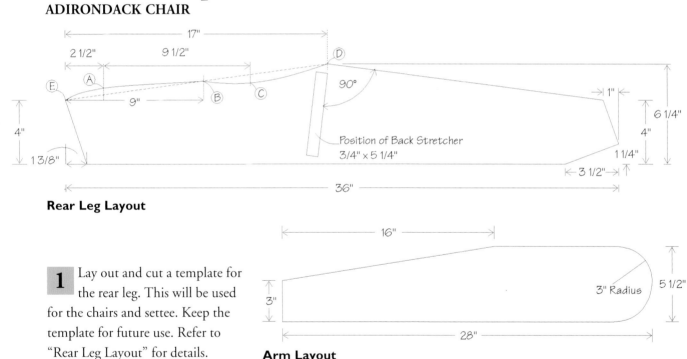

Rear Leg Layout

Arm Layout

1 Lay out and cut a template for the rear leg. This will be used for the chairs and settee. Keep the template for future use. Refer to "Rear Leg Layout" for details. Transfer the template to ¾″ stock and cut out two rear legs with a jigsaw or band saw.

2 Create a template for the chair and settee arms as detailed in "Arm Layout." Transfer the template to ¾″ stock and cut out two chair arms.

3 Clamp the pair of legs to-gether and sand smooth. Follow the same procedure with the arms.

4 Clamp the rear end of the back leg on a level surface so its foot is resting flat. The front top surface at point E in "Rear Leg Layout" should measure approximately 15″ from the level surface. The front face should be plumb.

5 Cut two front legs at ¾″ thick by 3½″ wide by 22″ long.

6 Attach the front legs to the back legs. The back leg is connected to the front leg with a 1″ setback as shown in "Leg Assembly." Secure the connection with waterproof, moisture-cured polyurethane glue and three 1¼″ exterior-grade screws.

Step 4

Step 6

Adirondack Chair		
Number	**Part**	**Dimensions** (**Thickness** × **Width** × **Length**)
2	Rear Legs	¾″ × 7¼″ × 36″
2	Arms	¾″ × 5½″ × 28″
2	Front Legs	¾″ × 3½″ × 22″
1	Front Stretcher	¾″ × 5¼″ × 22″
1	Back Stretcher	¾″ × 5¼″ × 20½″
8	Back Slats	¾″ × 2⁷⁄₁₆″ × 35⅞″
1	Back Brace	¾″ × 1½″ × 20½″
7	Seat Slats	¾″ × 2⁷⁄₁₆″ × 22″
1	Rear Arm Support	¾″ × 1½″ × 26″

To get these parts, you will need to find or purchase the following lumber and supplies:

Number	Nominal Stock Size	To Yield These Parts
1	1″ × 8″ × 8′	Back Legs, Front Legs
4	1″ × 6″ × 8′	Balance of Chair Components

7 Next, the two leg assemblies are joined with a front stretcher board. It measures ¾″ thick by 5¼″ wide by 22″ long. Use polyurethane glue on all contact points and screw two 2″ screws per side into ⅜″ counterbored holes that are filled with plugs.

8 Cut a back stretcher board measuring ¾″ thick by 5¼″ wide by 20½″ long. Position as shown in "Rear Leg Layout" with its back face in line with the high point on the rear leg. Use a square as shown so the stretcher board is at a 90° angle to the back leg surface. Glue and secure with two screws per side through the outside of the rear leg. Fill the counterbored holes with wood plugs and sand flush.

9 To strengthen and reduce twisting at the joints, corner blocks should be installed. They are wooden right triangles that are glued and screwed in place. Four blocks are required and attached as shown.

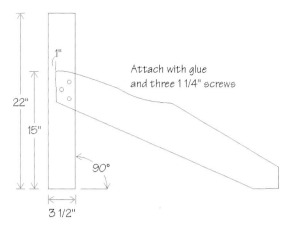

Leg Assembly

Step 8

Step 9

Step 10

Step 11

10 Eight back slats at ¾" thick by 2⁷⁄₁₆" wide by 35⅞" long are attached to the inside face of the back stretcher board. Use glue and two 1¼" screws per slat. They are spaced ⅛" apart and installed flush with the bottom edge of the back stretcher board. Leave a ¹⁄₁₆" space between the two end slats and the rear legs.

11 Cut and attach an upper back brace measuring ¾" thick by 1½" wide and 20½" long. The brace is secured 6" down from the top edge of the back slats with glue and one 1¼" screw per slat as illustrated. Maintain the ⅛" spacing between slats.

12 Clamp a scrap board to the chair's back slats from the rear so the board's center is 13" down from the top of the slats. Make a simple stick compass with a pencil and nail spaced at 13" apart. Scribe an arc on the chair back making sure that the nail point is centered across the width of the back slats. Cut with a jigsaw and sand the slats smooth.

13 Next, install seven seat slats at ¾" thick by 2⁷⁄₁₆" wide by 22" long. The slats are secured through the top to the back leg with 1½" screws in a counterbored hole. Apply polyurethane glue to the joints for added strength. Plug the screw holes with wood plugs so that the screw heads are covered. Begin installing the seat slats from the back with a ⅛" spacing between the boards. The front slat will overhang the front stretcher board. Add two extra screws through the front slat into the front stretcher board.

14 After installing the seat slats, you may find a spot where the slats' top surfaces aren't perfectly flush with each other. This may be due to a minor error in cutting the curved back leg. If that's the case, now is a good time to sand the seat contour smooth.

Step 12

Step 13

15 The rear arm support has to be cut at an angle to compensate for the slanted chair back. The simplest way to determine the angle is to clamp a scrap 1 × 2 to the back and use a level from on top of the front leg as shown. Mark the angle. Cut a ¾" by 1½" by 26"-long board and angle the top edge with a hand plane or table saw. Install the back arm support's top edge level with the front leg's top on both sides. Use one 1¼" screw per slat, installed from behind the chair.

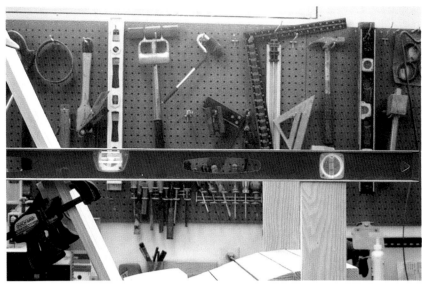

Step 15

16 Before securing the chair arms, two arm supports will be installed. These are simply wooden right triangles cut from 1 × 4 stock. Two sides are each 3½" long. The support blocks are secured with glue and two screws through the front leg. Verify that the top surface of the block is flush with the front leg's top surface. Center the support block on the front leg and use a square to hold it parallel to the edge of the front leg.

Step 16

17 Attach the arms with glue and two screws into the rear arm support and two into the front angled support. The arms are best secured with screws through the top into the supports. Counterbore the screw holes and fill the holes with plugs. To ensure proper arm alignment, clamp a ¾"-thick block to the inside surface of the front leg. Align the arms along the inside edge flush with this block. The back end of the arm is also flush with the back surface of the rear arm support.

18 Sand all surfaces smooth. Check that all of the wood plugs are flush.

Step 17

Construction Steps
ADIRONDACK SETTEE

The Adirondack settee is a wider version of the chair with a center seat support, which is nothing more than a shortened rear leg. All of the building principles that I used in constructing the chair will once again be used to build the settee.

1 Cut out two rear and front legs and assemble in the same manner as the chair.

2 We now need to join the leg assemblies with a front and rear stretcher board. Note that the length of these boards is not twice the length of the chair stretcher boards. We want to maintain a multiple of eight back slats. If we were to push two chairs together, we'd have two extra sets of legs in the middle. The width of those boards (four at ¾″ thick) must be subtracted. The front stretcher for the settee is ¾″ thick by 5¼″ wide by 42½″ long. The back stretcher board is ¾″ thick by 5¼″ wide by 41″ long. Attach these boards as previously detailed.

3 To support the added length of the seat slats, a center leg will be installed. This center support is the front part of the rear leg. Use the rear leg pattern to trace the support. The section required is from the front of the rear leg, which is point E to the front face of the back stretcher in "Rear Leg Layout" on page 89. Use the angled front face of the back stretcher as the cut line. Install with glue and two screws through the front and rear stretcher boards. Plug the counterbored screw holes.

Step 2

Step 3

Adirondack Settee		
Number	**Part**	**Dimensions (Thickness × Width × Length)**
2	Rear Legs	¾″ × 7¼″ × 36″
2	Front Legs	¾″ × 3½″ × 22″
1	Front Stretcher	¾″ × 5¼″ × 42½″
1	Back Stretcher	¾″ × 5¼″ × 41″
1	Center Leg	¾″ × 7¼″ × 17″
16	Back Slats	¾″ × 2⁷⁄₁₆″ × 35⅞″
1	Upper Back Brace	¾″ × 1½″ × 41″
7	Seat Slats	¾″ × 2⁷⁄₁₆″ × 42½″
2	Arms	¾″ × 5½″ × 28″
1	Rear Arm Support	¾″ × 1½″ × 46½″

To get these parts, you will need to find or purchase the following lumber and supplies:

Number	Nominal Stock Size	To Yield These Parts
1	1″ × 8″ × 8′	Rear Legs, Center Support
5	1″ × 6″ × 8′	Seat Slats, Front Stretcher, Upper Back Brace, Rear Arm Support
2	1″ × 6″ × 12′	Back Slats

4 Install four corner blocks in the same position as they were installed on the chair.

5 Cut and install 16 back boards at ¾″ thick by 2⁷⁄₁₆″ wide by 35⅞″ long. Repeat the installation procedures for the chair. A notch in one or possibly two of the back slats, depending on where you placed the center support, must be cut in order for the slat to fit around this support.

6 An upper back brace at ¾″ thick by 1½″ wide by 41″ long is required for the settee. As previously detailed, attach this brace 6″ from the top of the back boards with glue and one screw per back board.

7 Scribe two 13″ arcs to match the arc cut on the chair. Center one curve in the middle of eight back slats on the left side, 13″ down from the top, and one on the right side. The curved lines should meet in the center of the settee. Cut along the curved lines with a jigsaw and sand.

8 Cut and attach seven seat slats, each at ¾″ thick by 2⁷⁄₁₆″ wide by 42½″ long, with one screw in each leg and middle support. Drill and counterbore each screw hole and plug. Space the boards at ⅛″ to allow for water drainage. As with the chair, you may find one seat slat slightly higher or lower than the one beside it. If this situation occurs, sand the seat slats and contour smooth before installing the arms.

9 The arm support is ¾″ thick by 1½″ wide, with an angle cut at approximately 22½°, and 46½″ long. All of the remaining dimensions for the arms and exterior arm supports are the same as the chair. Attach the rear arm support, arms and front arm supports to the settee.

10 The settee is now complete and ready for final sanding and finishing.

Step 5

Step 7

Step 9

Construction Steps

ADIRONDACK COFFEE TABLE

The coffee table is built to match the chair and settee. Its design couldn't be simpler. A rectangular 1 × 4 frame with 1 × 4 legs. The top of the matching table uses the chair and settee back slat design with an arc at each end to match. It's easy to build and surprisingly strong. It really completes the set.

1 Form a box frame by joining two boards at ¾" thick by 3½" wide by 30" long with two end boards at ¾" thick by 3½" wide by 16" long. (See "Box Frame.") The outside measurement after assembly should be 31½" long by 16" wide. Attach the boards with screws in counterbored holes and fill with wood plugs.

2 Install a center board that's ¾" thick by 3½" wide by 14½" long.

3 Install four corner blocks cut from 1 × 4 stock as shown.

4 Install four legs ¾" thick by 3½" wide by 15¼" long to the outside corners of the table frame. Attach the legs so the end grains on the short frame boards are covered. Apply glue and insert three 1¼" screws from the inside of the frame.

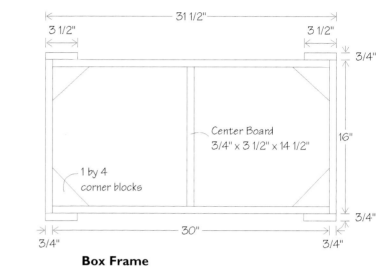

31 1/2"
3 1/2"   3 1/2"   3/4"
Center Board
3/4" x 3 1/2" x 14 1/2"   16"
1 by 4
corner blocks   3/4"
30"
3/4"   3/4"

Box Frame

Step 3

Coffee Table		
Number	**Part**	**Dimensions (Thickness × Width × Length)**
2	Frame Ends	¾" × 3½" × 16"
2	Frame Sides	¾" × 3½" × 30"
1	Center Board	¾" × 3½" × 14½"
4	Legs	¾" × 3½" × 15¼"
8	Top Boards	¾" × 2¼" × 42"

To get these parts, you will need to find or purchase the following lumber and supplies:

Number	Nominal Stock Size	To Yield These Parts
2	1" × 4" × 8'	Frame, Center Support, Legs
2	1" × 6" × 8'	Tabletop Boards

Step 4

5 Cut and attach eight tabletop boards at ¾" thick by 2¼" wide by 42" long. Four boards are installed on each side of the center with ⅛" spacing. Drill and counterbore a screw hole through the top of the boards, one at each end and one into the center board. Fill the holes with wood plugs and sand smooth.

6 Draw a 13" arc on each end with the stick compass and cut. The table is now ready for final sanding and finishing.

Step 5

Construction Notes

When you're building lawn furniture, particularly chairs, it's important to cover the screw heads with wood plugs. People tend to wear less clothes in the summer months and bare skin can come into contact with hot exposed screw heads. It isn't pleasant and can be dangerous.

Covering screw heads with wood plugs also helps prolong the life of the furniture. Quite often, even the best of exterior screws rust and infect the wood. If you've ever taken apart an old deck with steel screws and nails, you've seen that the point of failure is at the rusted nail. Plugging the screw heads seals the metal in the wood, protecting them from the weather.

Adirondack furniture continues to be one of the most popular projects to build and use. I've seen chairs that are over twenty years old and still being used. These long-lasting chairs were obviously built with care and attention to detail with respect to weather conditions. That's why they've lasted so long.

Consider building your set out of hardwood and stainless steel fasteners. It's a little more expensive, but that cost stretched over ten or fifteen years is very reasonable.

Take a little extra time finishing this furniture. There are a lot of places where water and dirt can build up, so the finish is important. Three, possibly four coats of a high-quality outdoor stain is well worth the expense.

Variations and Options

The Adirondack-style chair is based on a contoured seat and sloped back. There are a few style variations, but most pieces can readily be identified as Adirondack furniture. However, the back of the chair can be sloped more or less than shown. The seat's contour can also be altered to suit your personal taste.

Which wood species should you use to build these chairs? That's always a consideration based on intended use and available budget. Some of the specialty woods like teak and mahogany are expensive, so use the materials list and compare the cost of different species in your area.

Many early examples of the Adirondack chair were constructed of hard pine or maple. Wood that at one time was inexpensive and plentiful is more costly today. Materials cost is an important consideration. However, take a look at the materials list. There isn't a large amount of material needed for each piece.

Personally, I like ash, maple or birch. All of these woods are easily finished and hold a screw well. They all have a relatively tight grain structure, which produces a nice, smooth surface after sanding and finishing.

Adirondack furniture is fun to build. There aren't any overly complicated joints and the completed project brings a lot of satisfaction. Decide on the style variations, pick the wood and build a few pieces for your home or cottage. You'll be pleased with the results.

CHAPTER 12

Garden Arbors

Walk-Through Arbor

Seated Arbor

Arbors have been a part of our landscape projects for hundreds of years. They come in all shapes and serve to define a pathway or provide a quiet spot to rest as well as support beautiful vines.

Two styles of arbors are detailed in this chapter. The walk-through and seated types allowed us to feature two different designs, although either can be used with or without a seat. Many of the gardeners I spoke with wanted an arbor as an accent feature or to divide two areas of a garden. The other requirement was a lattice designed into the arbor that would allow a vine to climb. The grid or lattice detail is important and depends a great deal on the type of vine grown. It's wise to consider the plant's "climbing requirement" before completing your design.

Rather than building a flattop walk-through arbor, I opted for something with a bit of flare. The top of the arbor is cut from 2 × 10 lumber with spaced 2 × 2s. It's a unique design that's received many favorable comments. And, surprisingly, it's very simple to build. I've used this arbor as the gateway into a secluded cedar grove. Because of this, the wood choice was obvious: construction-grade cedar.

There was also the issue of portability because the arbor may have to be moved temporarily to complete major maintenance in the grove. For this reason, I drove wooden stakes into the ground and secured them to the arbor sides with exterior wood screws. This arbor design isn't overly heavy and doesn't have a large, flat surface that can be caught in the wind.

The seated arbor was built on-site, with the exception of the side grids. They were much easier to fabricate in the shop with a radial arm saw. Pressure-treated lumber was my wood of choice because the structure was being painted. You'll notice in the photographs that it's surrounded by heavy green foliage. If the arbor was painted anything but white, it would have almost disappeared.

There was also some concern about permanently anchoring the legs, so I decided to use ground spikes. This was the first time I've used this method and was pleased with the results. Of course, if you live in a climate that doesn't experience frost, just about any support system will be fine. In my area, frost three feet deep into the earth is a fact of life.

I haven't had an opportunity to build many arbors in my renovation business. Most homeowners and woodworkers can easily handle these projects with a little guidance, and I, too, enjoyed designing and building these two structures. It was amazing to see how much they improved the landscape. An arbor project is worth the time and money spent.

The dimensions, while accurate, are given as a guideline only because each location has very specific size requirements. However, both designs can easily be altered to custom fit any situation.

Walk-Through Arbor

Number	Part	Dimensions (Thickness × Width × Length)
8	Uprights	1½″ × 3½″ × 84″
8	Cross Braces	¾″ × 1½″ × 24″
1	Lattice Grid	4′ × 8′
2	Barrel Arches	1½″ × 8⅝″ × 43″
17	Roof Boards	1½″ × 1½″ × 31¼″
4	Face Boards	¾″ × 3½″ × 80″

To get these parts, you will need to find or purchase the following lumber and supplies:

Number	Nominal Stock Size	To Yield These Parts
8	2″ × 4″ × 8′	Frame
2	1″ × 2″ × 8′	Cross Braces
1	4′ × 8′	Lattice Grid
1	2″ × 10″ × 8′	Arch
6	2″ × 2″ × 8′	Roof Boards
4	1″ × 4″ × 8′	Face Boards

Construction Steps
WALK-THROUGH ARBOR

1 Eight boards at 1½″ thick by 3½″ wide by 84″ long are required to build the framework.

2 Cut a rabbet and dado in each of the eight boards as shown in "Frame Layout." This is best accomplished with a dado blade on the radial arm saw. However, a router or handsaw and chisel can also be used.

3 Cut eight cross braces at ¾″ thick by 1½″ wide by 24″ long.

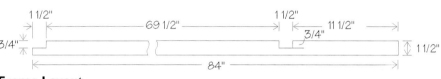

Frame Layout

Step 2

4 Assemble each of the four wall halves as shown in "Wall Half Assembly." Exterior construction adhesive and one 1¼" exterior screw per joint were used to secure the connections.

5 Rip a 4' × 8' sheet of lattice to form two pieces of approximately 24" × 72".

6 Assemble the wall sections, sandwiching the lattice between two half walls as shown. The lattice sheets are flush with the top of each wall section. Use construction adhesive and 3" screws.

7 If you plan to use construction-grade cedar, now is an ideal time to sand the walls.

8 Lay out two barrel arches on two pieces of 2 × 10 stock as shown in "Barrel Arch Layout." Cut the arches with a jigsaw.

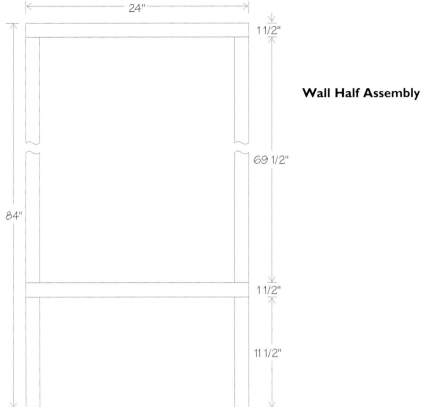

Wall Half Assembly

24"
1 1/2"
69 1/2"
84"
1 1/2"
11 1/2"

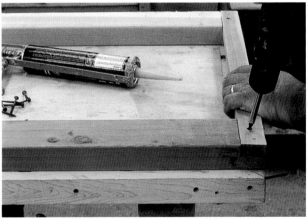

Step 4

Step 6

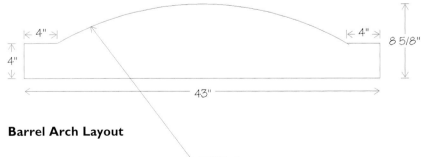

4"
4"
4"
8 5/8"
43"

Barrel Arch Layout

36" Radius

Step 8

9 Clamp both arches together and sand.

10 Place both wall sections on their edges at 43″ apart. Attach one barrel arch flush with the outside wall edges and even with the top as shown. The arches were attached using polyurethane glue and four 3″ screws per side that had the screw holes plugged.

11 The arbor will eventually be moved to the garden site, so now is a good time to attach two bottom supports on the front and rear. These supports can be made from any scrap lumber and are screwed to the underside of the walls, so they are at the same spacing as the tops of the walls.

12 Carefully flip the arbor onto the other side and attach the second barrel arch in the same manner as the first.

Step 10

Step 12

Step 16

13 Block the arbor so it sits 2″ off the floor. Cut 17 boards for the roof at 1½″ × 1½″ × 31¼″. Sand and round over all edges with a ¼″ roundover bit.

14 Lay out the roof boards, spacing them at 1½″ apart. Equalize the front and back overhang, which should be about 2⅛″. For a balanced look, the first and last space should be equalized. However, curve variances when cutting the barrel arch may alter your spac-

ing. To equalize the outside spaces, attach a roof board in the center of the arch. Then mark layout lines toward each side with a 1½″ space between the boards. Measure the last space on each side and equalize.

15 Attach the roof boards at each end with construction adhesive and a 3″ screw in pre-drilled holes.

16 Secure the last two roof boards to the arbor sides, level with the bottom edge of the barrel arch.

17 Four face boards at ¾″ thick by 3½″ wide by 80″ long will be used to cover the front and back faces of the arbor. Install each of the four boards with construction adhesive and nails. Center the boards on each face. The exposure (reveal) of the 2 × 4s on each side of the face board will vary depending on the thickness of the latticework.

18 The arbor is ready to be transported to the site for installation. For the present, leave the straps attached to the bottom to prevent damage to the framework.

19 Level the ground and place the arbor. Verify that the wall-to-wall space at the bottom equals the top spacing.

20 Drive two foot stakes into the ground beside the arbor and secure to the frame with 3″ screws. As previously discussed, my arbor can be moved if necessary. If yours is to be permanently placed, anchor the frame to concrete piers with the appropriate hardware.

21 As you install each stake and anchor the arbor, verify that the sides are plumb.

22 The arbor is now ready for a clear finish or stain. By strategically placing plants at the base of the arbor, the support stakes disappear.

Step 18

Step 20

Step 21

Construction Steps

SEATED ARBOR

1 To build our grid panels, start by cutting eight vertical members at 1½″ × 1½″ × 68″ long and 16 horizontal members at 1½″ × 1½″ × 27″.

2 Clamp the vertical members together and mark layout lines for the dado and rabbet cuts. Cut the dadoes.

3 Clamp and mark the layout lines for the horizontal members. Cut the grooves with a dado blade on the radial arm saw. Use a 1 × 2 piece of stock to lock the members while cutting the joints.

4 Assemble the grid frames as shown in "Grid Frame Layout." Use 2″ outdoor-rated screws and construction adhesive on the outside vertical members. Begin the assembly process by securing eight horizontal members to two outside vertical members. Next, install the two inside vertical members into their corresponding dado joints. Use construction adhesive and a brad nail at all half-lap dado joints.

Step 3

Step 4

Note: All dadoes and rabbets are 3/4" deep

Grid Frame Layout

Seated Arbor		
Number	Part	Dimensions (Thickness × Width × Length)
8	Grid Stiles	1½″ × 1½″ × 68″
16	Grid Rails	1½″ × 1½″ × 27″
4	Posts	3½″ × 3½″ × 84″
2	Face Boards	1½″ × 5½″ × 64″
2	Upper Side Boards	1½″ × 5½″ × 35½″
7	Roof Trusses	1½″ × 5½″ × 47″
1	Front Seat Support	1½″ × 3½″ × 51″
2	Seat Supports	1½″ × 3½″ × 20″
2	Legs	1½″ × 3½″ × 16½″
2	Back Supports	1½″ × 3½″ × 16″
10	Seat and Back Slats	1½″ × 3½″ × 46″
2	Arms	1½″ × 3½″ × 28½″

To get these parts, you will need to find or purchase the following lumber and supplies:

Number	Nominal Stock Size	To Yield These Parts
4	2″ × 6″ × 8′	Grid
4	4″ × 4″ × 8′	Posts
6	2″ × 6″ × 8′	Face Boards, Upper Side Boards, Roof Trusses
8	2″ × 4″ × 8′	Seat, Arms
4		Post Spikes

5 At the site, stake and string a frame pattern to locate the post spikes as shown in "Post Spike Locations." Measure the diagonals of the string frame to ensure they are equal, which means the corners are at right angles to each other.

6 Install the post spikes using a scrap piece of 4 × 4. Verify that the posts are level with each other and plumb.

7 Install one 3½" × 3½" × 84"-long post in each spike. Plumb each post, verify that the dimensions shown in "Post Spike Locations" are correct and tighten the posts in place. Temporarily attach cross bracing to the posts to keep them in position while the remaining frame members are attached. Secure each grid panel to the posts with 3" screws. I installed the grid panels 12" above the ground.

8 Cut a front and rear face board as shown in "Face Board Layout." They extend past each side of the arbor posts by 5¼". Temporarily attach them 1" above the post tops with nails on the outside front and back faces of the arbor frame. Level the face boards across the front and to each other.

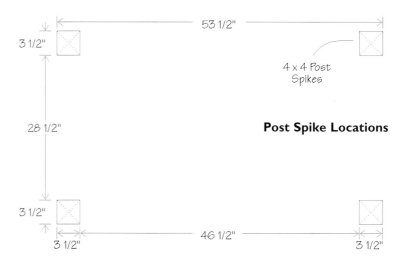

Post Spike Locations

Step 5

Face Board Layout

Step 6

Step 8

9 Cut and attach two upper side boards at 1½″ thick by 5½″ wide by 35½″ long. These can also be temporarily attached with nails. Hold them flush with the tops of the front and rear face boards.

10 Check that the arbor frame posts are plumb and the cross boards are level. Once you are satisfied, install ⅜″ × 3″ lag bolts and washers at each corner. Two per joint are required for a total of 16 bolts.

11 Cut seven roof trusses. Notch the trusses as detailed to fit over the front and rear face boards (see "Roof Truss Layout").

12 Center the first board on the front and rear face. Secure with 3″ wood screws from behind the front and rear face boards into the truss. Install the two outside trusses tight to the outer faces of each post. Attach the remaining four trusses between the outside and center truss with equal spacing. I calculated a distance of approximately 7 ⅝″ between trusses on the project arbor.

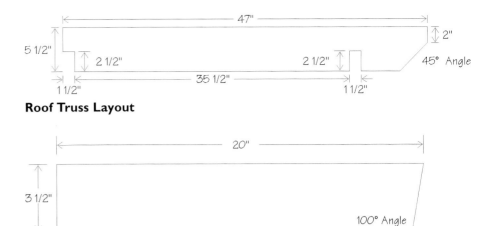

Roof Truss Layout

Seat Support Layout

Step 9

Step 11

Step 12

13 To build a seat, cut a front support at $1\frac{1}{2}'' \times 3\frac{1}{2}'' \times 51''$. The length can vary depending on where the grid frames are screwed to the posts (measure between the outside faces of the grid). Screw the seat board to the grid frame at 15″ off the ground. This board is attached behind the second vertical member of the grid. Cut two seat supports as shown in "Seat Support Layout" on page 105, and two legs at $1\frac{1}{2}'' \times 3\frac{1}{2}'' \times 16\frac{1}{2}''$. Assemble as shown in "Seat Assembly."

14 Cut two back supports at $1\frac{1}{2}'' \times 3\frac{1}{2}'' \times 16''$. These supports are secured to the top of the seat supports and at the point of contact with the rear arbor posts. Since the seat supports have a 10° drop, the back supports will have a 10° rear slant. See "Seat Assembly."

15 Ten seat and back slats at $1\frac{1}{2}'' \times 3\frac{1}{2}'' \times 46''$ are required. Start securing the back slats from the bottom with ⅛″ spacing. Attach the seat slats from back to front with ⅛″ spacing.

16 I decided to add two simple arms at $1\frac{1}{2}'' \times 3\frac{1}{2}'' \times 28\frac{1}{2}''$. The back of the arm was cut at 10° to match the back slant and the front was rounded over with a belt sander. Secure the arms to the grid members with screws through the grid and bench back slats.

17 If you are going to leave it unpainted, it would be wise to dress all of the exposed wood cuts with pressure-treated, end cut treatment. If you plan to paint the arbor, do it as soon as possible so that all open cuts are protected.

Seat Assembly

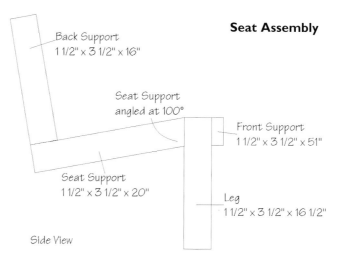

Back Support
1 1/2" x 3 1/2" x 16"

Seat Support
angled at 100°

Front Support
1 1/2" x 3 1/2" x 51"

Seat Support
1 1/2" x 3 1/2" x 20"

Leg
1 1/2" x 3 1/2" x 16 1/2"

Side View

Step 13

Step 16

Construction Notes

It's a simple matter to permanently anchor either of these arbor designs. Add the necessary length to each of the four main legs and cement in place. Or pour concrete piers and attach the arbor legs with metal brackets.

Construction-grade cedar was used for the walk-through arbor and pressure-treated spruce for the seated arbor. As with all wood used outdoors, protection is necessary if the life of the wood is to be maximized. Clear-coat the cedar with a preservative and apply end cut dressing to the pressure-treated lumber.

All hardware used should be rated as outdoor material. Steel fasteners will rust and begin a rapid decay process in the wood. Even though the hardware is exterior-rated, apply extra coats of finish.

Joints and ends of lumber tend to hold water and dirt. These areas are the first to begin deteriorating. It's worth the time and expense to protect them. If you see an area that has poor drainage, drill release holes and coat the holes with finish. This extra attention to potential problem areas will add years to the life of your outdoor projects.

In many cases, your arbor project will remain outside on a permanent basis. Unlike a garden chair that can be stored for the winter months, arbors spend their useful life exposed to all of the seasons. It's another reason why protection is such an important issue.

Variations and Options

Either of the two project arbors can be altered to suit your needs. Dimensional changes in width or length can easily be managed with a few simple calculations.

The sizes of my project arbors were driven by existing conditions and requirements. This situation is common and will probably be necessary when you're planning to build. Wood choice is a matter of personal taste. Just about any species is suitable. During my research for arbor projects, I surprisingly found that painted, pressure-treated wood was a popular choice.

The walk-through arbor project can easily be made into a seated arbor, and the seated arbor can be used as a walk-through style. The grid work can be interchanged to accommodate vine requirements.

The seated arbor is commonly built with a back grid to increase the privacy. Mine was built in an area that backed onto dense foliage, so the back wasn't necessary. However, you may need to add back lattice or a grid if your location is in the open and you want more privacy.

One of the best applications I've seen was an arbor used as part of a fence that had a gate built into the frame. It was a beautiful application and added a great deal of visual appeal to the landscape. Arbors can add so much to the "street appeal" of a home. There's nothing more inviting than an arbor as a gated entrance to your backyard.

The applications are endless for these beautiful and functional landscape accent projects. I hope you get as much enjoyment from building yours as I did with these two projects.

CHAPTER 13

Building the Classic Gazebo

Have you ever considered building a gazebo in your backyard? Does it seem like a complicated and intimidating project? Well, here's a hexagon gazebo plan that's beautiful and easy to build.

The most complicated issue with any structure that has a roof is fabricating the roof rafters. It can be a task that tests your patience, but I'll detail how easy it is to calculate common rafter dimensions before we start building.

The other area that seems difficult to many woodworkers is the process of installing cedar shingles or shakes. Installing these shingles is no doubt an art, but there is plenty of information available to guide you through the process. I'll discuss the process and talk about where to get accurate data before you start building your gazebo.

My project gazebo was constructed on an existing concrete pad. These patio stones had been in place for many years, so I was confident that it was a stable base. However, the gazebo can be built on newly installed concrete piers or 2′-square patio stones that are laid on stable ground.

Cedar is the classic wood of choice for these structures, but they can be built with any wood. This design is easily adapted to pressure-treated wood construction with a metal or asphalt shingle roof.

The hexagon-style gazebo follows a basic mathematical principal.

Every regular polygon (or multiple-sided object that has equal sides and equal angles) fits within a circle. Therefore, when constructing the shape, you will "travel" in a circle or 360° (see the tip on "Figuring Angles"). The hexagon is comprised of six equal sides with six equal angles of 120°. So all of the angle cuts where two boards join will be at 60° per board which, when joined, form a 120° angle.

My gazebo has a diameter of approximately 8′, which was the requirement for this site. However, don't feel that you're restricted to this size. The structure can be altered to suit your site. It's simply a matter of adjusting the rim joist lengths to increase or decrease the hexagon. Changing the size affects all of the measurements, particularly the roof rafter length. This seems like a complicated process, but I'll detail how the common roof rafter length is determined. It's an easy-to-use, straightforward, mathematical formula.

Building your own gazebo will save you hundreds of dollars. The material cost is relatively low compared to the labor cost. Contractor-built gazebos tend to be expensive because of the unusually high amount of time needed to build these structures. They're not easily mass produced and require a lot of time cutting angles. Unlike a straightforward deck, gazebo construction requires slow, patient assembly and cutting. Because you provide the labor, the construction cost becomes very attractive.

However, with all of this talk about angles and construction time, I've forgotten the most important issue: A gazebo is a unique and beautiful addition to any property. It's a wonderful retreat in your own backyard that provides shade, protection from the rain and a secluded spot to relax and enjoy a great book or entertain friends.

Cedar Shakes and Shingles

There is a wealth of information available about cedar shake and shingle products from the Cedar Shake and Shingle Bureau. You can contact them at 515 116th Avenue NE, Suite 275, Bellevue, Washington 98004-5294. The Bureau's telephone number is (206) 453-1323 and its Web site is http://www.cedarbureau.org.

Shingles and shakes are virtually the same with one exception. Cedar shingles are sawn and shakes are split. The shingle has a smooth surface and the shake has a textured grain appearance.

Shingles and shakes are normally applied over spaced roof sheathing. If the shingle exposure—the amount visible after the next row is installed—is 6″, then the sheathing or roof boards are spaced at 6″ on center.

In most cases, such as our project gazebo, 1 × 4 boards are used for roof sheathing. By making the on-center spacing of the roof boards equal the shingle exposure, we will be nailing each shingle in the center of a board.

Installation of cedar roofs on houses is a bit more involved than covering an outdoor structure. Residential and commercial applications must deal with eave protection, ice dams, heat loss and water damage. For these and other reasons, added measures such as the installation of roof felt and other materials are standard practices. Obviously, heat loss isn't a concern with our project, but rain protection is an issue that demands a properly installed roof.

Here are a few of the generally accepted procedures to follow when installing cedar shingles and shakes.

- The starter course is two layers of shingles.
- Butt ends of the starter course should project 1½″ beyond the fascia.
- Spacing between shakes should be a minimum of ⅜″ to a maximum of ⅝″. Shingles should be spaced a minimum of ¼″ and a maximum of ⅜″.
- Joints between shakes and shingles should be separated by at least 1½″ from overlaid rows.
- Nails are placed 1″ from the shingles side edges and only two nails per shingle are required. Nails should be driven flush with the shingle surface without crushing the face.
- The use of corrosion-resistant nails is recommended.
- Intersecting roofs and hips are capped with alternately overlapping shingles. The exposure is the same as used on the roof, and the shingles are cut to a width of 4″ to 5″.

There are some interesting facts about cedar roofs that are well worth considering. Although more costly than traditional asphalt roofs, cedar shingle roofs tend to last considerably longer and therefore justify the added expense.

Cedar shingles have a degree of structural integrity and add to the strength of a building. Cedar roofs are suited for a wide range of climatic conditions, and many of the cedar products on the market today have decay-resistant coatings.

There are many benefits to using cedar shingles or shakes for the gazebo roof. However, there is the issue of cost and you may want to investigate the price difference between asphalt and cedar shingles in your area.

In my part of the country, cedar shingles and shakes are five times the price of asphalt. That can be a substantial figure if your gazebo is large. I used four bundles of cedar shingles with each bundle covering 30 square feet at a 7½″ exposure.

In the final analysis, you are saving hundreds of dollars by building the gazebo yourself, so the added expense of a cedar roof may very well be justified.

Common Rafter Calculations

If you plan on building the project gazebo, common rafter calculations will not be required; simply cut the rafters as shown. However, if you change the dimensions, you'll have to determine the new common rafter size. Don't let the following explanation confuse you—it's very simple. We'll take it one step at a time.

First, it's necessary to understand some of the common terms associated with roof framing. Refer to "Common Roofing Terms" as the terms are discussed.

- The **span** of a roof is the horizontal distance covered by a roof. The measurement is taken from the outside faces of the wall framing.
- A **rafter** is one of the sloping members of a roof frame.

- The **total run** of a rafter is the horizontal distance over which it rises.
- The **total rise** is the vertical distance that the roof rises.
- The **ridge** is the top of the roof where the rafters meet.
- The **line length** of a rafter is the longest side of a right triangle, called the hypotenuse, which is formed by the line length, total rise and total run.
- The **pitch** is the amount in inches that the roof rises for every foot of run in the total run. In "Common Roofing Terms," the roof rises 4″ for every foot of total run. Therefore, the roof is said to have a 4/12 pitch.

There are rafter terms worth detailing that will make

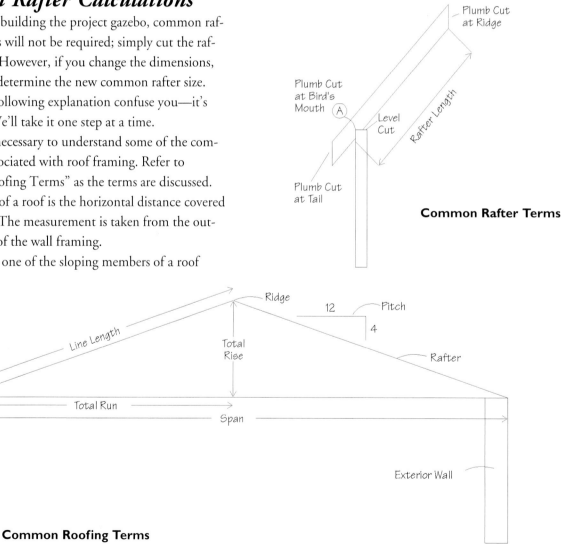

Common Rafter Terms

Common Roofing Terms

the explanations simpler. Refer to "Common Rafter Terms" on the previous page.

- A **plumb cut** is any cut on a rafter that is vertical when the rafter is in position.
- A **level cut** is any cut on the rafter that is level when the rafter is in position.
- The **bird's mouth** of a rafter is the combination of a plumb and level cut. This combination cut rests on top of the wall plate.

The figure calculated for rafter length is measured from point A to point B as shown in "Common Rafter Terms." The same measurement will result if we measure along the top or middle of the rafter as long as we properly extend the plumb cut at the bird's mouth. But for ease of explanation, measure the rafter length as shown.

To determine the rafter length for any given structure, we use a mathematical formula that applies to any triangle with a 90° (or right) angle. It states that the sum of the squares for the two shorter sides (our total run and total rise) equals the square of the hypotenuse (or longest side). In "Figure Rafter Length," A squared plus B squared equals C squared. The dimensions used apply to the project gazebo.

The total run is 45¼″ or half the span as detailed in "Common Roofing Terms." This dimension is half the distance from outside wall to outside wall along the rafter path. With respect to a hexagon gazebo, our rafter path is from post to post. The total rise is calculated by deciding the pitch or slope of the roof. I decided on a roof for this gazebo that had a 4/12 pitch. Therefore, my total rise (in inches) is the total run (also in inches) times the pitch. Remember, the pitch of the roof is stated as the number of inches that the roof rises for every foot (12 inches) of run. My roof rises 4″ for every 12 inches of run, so the number of running feet equals the total run divided by 12. See "Figuring Your Total Rise."

We now know that the common rafter for the project gazebo is 47¾″ long, measured from the ridge plumb cut to the bird's mouth plumb cut. It's important to standardize the rafter layout measurement, so mark two points at 47¾″ from point A to point B as shown in "Common Rafter Terms."

Two other layout lines are required to mark a com-

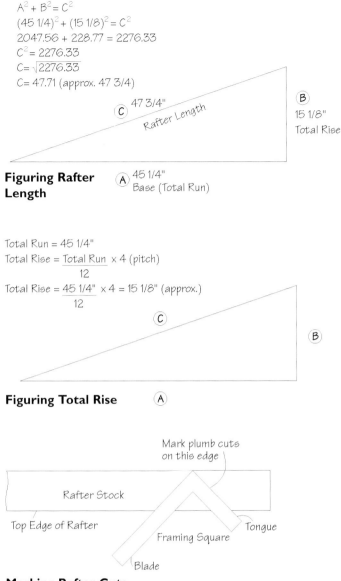

$$A^2 + B^2 = C^2$$
$$(45\ 1/4)^2 + (15\ 1/8)^2 = C^2$$
$$2047.56 + 228.77 = 2276.33$$
$$C^2 = 2276.33$$
$$C = \sqrt{2276.33}$$
$$C = 47.71 \text{ (approx. 47 3/4)}$$

C 47 3/4″ Rafter Length
B 15 1/8″ Total Rise

Figuring Rafter Length A 45 1/4″ Base (Total Run)

Total Run = 45 1/4″
$$\text{Total Rise} = \frac{\text{Total Run}}{12} \times 4 \text{ (pitch)}$$
$$\text{Total Rise} = \frac{45\ 1/4″}{12} \times 4 = 15\ 1/8″ \text{ (approx.)}$$

Figuring Total Rise

Mark plumb cuts on this edge
Rafter Stock
Top Edge of Rafter
Framing Square
Tongue
Blade

Marking Rafter Cuts

mon rafter for the gazebo. First, we have to determine the plumb cut angle and second, the depth of the bird's mouth plumb cut.

The second issue is the simplest and common to all rafters. Each carpenter has his or her own formula for the depth of the bird's mouth plumb cut. However, the most important factor is leaving enough material above the bird's mouth so as not to weaken the rafter tail. The rafter tail, that portion extending past the outside wall frame, often supports a portion of the roof as well as the fascia and soffit boards. My rule is to cut the bird's mouth plumb cut one third of the rafter's width. A 5½″ common rafter would have a 1¾″-deep bird's mouth.

The three common rafter plumb cuts at the ridge,

bird's mouth and rafter tail are the same angle. They are all "plumb" when the rafter is in its position. The simplest way to mark these cuts is to use a framing square.

To mark the plumb cuts with a framing square, lay the square on the side of the stock to the far right end. Hold the tongue of the square (short, thin part) with your right hand and the blade (wide, long part of the square) with your left hand. The inside of the square and the top edge of the rafter should face you as shown in "Marking Rafter Cuts" on page 111.

Hold the square so the 4″ mark on the inside of the tongue and the 12″ mark on the inside of the blade line up with the edge of the rafter stock. Mark along the outside edge of the tongue. That line is the ridge plumb cut for a 4/12 pitch roof.

Move the square to the first mark at A, "Common Rafter Terms," which in our case is 47¾″ away. Line it up in the same fashion as the ridge cut and mark the plumb cut for the bird's mouth. Measure up 1¾″ on the bird's mouth plumb cut, and draw a mark to the bottom edge of the rafter at right angles to the plumb cut, toward the ridge. That line is the bird's mouth level cut, which rests on top of the wall.

Finally, holding the framing square in the 4/12 position, out 12″ from the bird's mouth plumb cut, draw a plumb line for the rafter tail. This 12″ rafter tail figure is one of choice. The length of the rafter tail can be any dimension and is dependent on the roof style.

Most roof hand framing with common rafters has a ridge board. It runs along the center of the roof and is used to hold the rafters plumb. The gazebo also has a ridge board, which is referred to as a key block.

I'll discuss how the key block is cut and installed later in this chapter. However, since the common rafters meet at a ridge board, the length of the rafter must be adjusted to account for the space taken up by the ridge board. Each common rafter is cut back half the thickness of the ridge board or key block. The cut is made parallel to each common rafter's ridge plumb cut.

There's one rule worth remembering that will help you avoid mistakes. Always verify that plumb cuts are parallel to each other, and the bird's mouth level cut is at a right angle to the plumb cut before you saw the rafter.

It takes a little time and patience to complete and cut the first rafter, but that one becomes a template that

can be used to mark other rafters. After you've completed the cutting for the first two rafters, fit them in place to ensure they are correct.

Angle Verification

There's one golden rule that has to be followed when building any structure with walls. Remember, the angles where the walls meet must be accurate for the design of the building. For example, when framing a house, the diagonals are measured to ensure square corners. If the measurements are equal, the building is not "racked."

When building a six-sided structure, the distance from opposite posts must all be equal as illustrated in "Post Layout." If they are equal, we know that all of the angles where each wall joins another is at 120°.

Imagine shortening the distance between two opposite posts. That will change the angle of intersection on all of the walls, some will be greater than 120° and others will be less. If the distances between opposite posts aren't equal, all other measurements are affected. And the rafters, which are all cut based on three identical total span distances, will not fit properly.

Keep this rule in mind when building the gazebo. It's an important issue. As you'll see in the photographs, I blocked the post-to-post distances with three boards of the same length to keep the wall angles correct. The blocks were removed when they were in my way and replaced a few times during the construction.

Figuring Angles for Regular Polygons

To figure out the angle to cut each side for a regular polygon (a multisided object with equal sides and equal angles), follow this formula:

1. Divide 360 by the number of sides. For a hexagon, divide 360 by 6; you get 60.
2. Subtract the answer from 180°. This is the angle between the sides. For a hexagon, subtract 60 from 180; you get 120.
3. Divide this number by 2. This is the angle of the final piece. For a hexagon, divide 120 by 2; you get 60. Your final piece should have a point measuring 60°.

Construction Steps

I believe that all of my measurements are accurate, but suggest that you double check the dimensions given before you cut each piece. Slight variances in wood sizes in different areas, as well as differences due to assembly and placement procedures, may slightly alter the dimensions. Use the sizes given as a reference, and check measurements as the construction progresses.

1 Cut six rim joists at 1½" thick by 5½" wide by 40" long. Both ends of the joists are cut at a 30° angle.

2 Attach the six joists to six posts that are 3½" square by 96" long, shown as A in "Joist Layout" on page 114. Use 3" exterior wood screws in predrilled holes. The inside face of each joist should be attached flush with the inside face of each post.

3 Six upper support boards cut at 1½" × 3½" × 41¾" with a 30° angle on both ends are attached flush with the tops of the posts. Hold the outside edge of the support board flush with the outside edge of the posts. Verify the support board dimension by measuring the outside corner-to-corner distance of two posts at the bottom of the posts. These are now fixed in place by the rim joists and the top distance should equal the bottom distance to ensure the posts are plumb.

Gazebo

Number	Part	Dimensions (Thickness × Width × Length)
6	Posts	3½" × 3½" × 96"
6	Rim Joists	1½" × 5½" × 40"
6	Upper Supports	1½" × 3½" × 41¾"
4	Floor Joists	1½" × 5½" × 73¼"
2	Cross Joists	1½" × 5½" × 22⅛"
4	Angle Joists	1½" × 5½" × 23½"
6	Skirt Boards	1½" × 5½" × 47½"
16	Decking	1¼" × 6" × 8'
10	Upper and Lower Rails	1½" × 3½" × 41"
5	Rail Caps	1½" × 3½" × 41¾"
6	Top Plates	1½" × 3½" × 46"
1	Key Block	4" × 4" × 18"
6	Common Rafters	1½" × 5½" × 58¼"
2	Hexagon Blocks	1½" × 8" × 8"

To get these parts, you will need to find or purchase the following lumber and supplies:

Number	Nominal Stock Size	To Yield These Parts
6	4" × 4" × 8'	Posts
14	2" × 6" × 8'	Rim Joists, Joists, Common Rafters
14	2" × 4" × 8'	Upper Support Boards, Railing, Wall Plate
3	2" × 6" × 8'	Cedar Skirt
16	5/4 × 6" × 8'	Cedar Deck
1	4" × 4" × 18"	Key Block
1	2" × 4" × 18"	Hexagon Block
3	2" × 4" × 10'	Fascia
15	1" × 4" × 8'	Roof Sheathing, Railing Molding
17	1" × 4" × 8'	V-Groove Panel for Railing
4	Bundles	Cedar Shingles

Step 2

Step 3

4 Check that the cross dimensions as shown in "Post Layout" are equal. My dimension was 73¼". Cut four floor joists at 1½" thick by 5½" wide by 73¼" long, and install joists B as shown in "Joist Layout" at 12" centers.

5 Once the joists are attached, recheck the cross dimensions. It may be difficult to get an accurate post-to-post measurement, so mark the center point of each rim joist and measure from those reference points.

6 Install two cross joists, which for the project gazebo measured 1½" thick by 5½" wide by 22⅛" long from post to floor joist shown as C in "Joist Layout."

7 Four angle joists, item D in "Joist Layout," are cut and attached. These joists are cut at 30° on both ends and are 1½" thick by 5½" wide by 23½" long between the widest lines of the angle cuts.

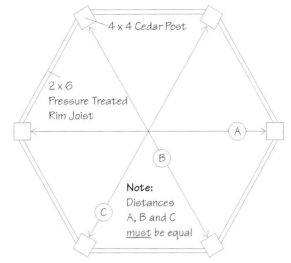

Post Layout

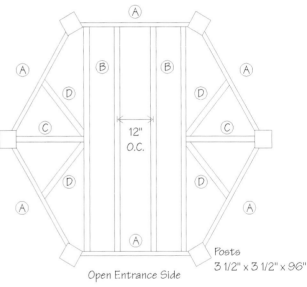

Joist Layout

Step 4

Step 5

Step 7

8 Cut six cedar skirt boards at 1½″ thick by 5½″ wide by 47½″ long, which are angle cut at 30° on each end. The measurement given is from outside angle to outside angle.

9 The next step in the construction process is to cut and attach the deck boards. For the project deck, I used five quarter (5/4) cedar decking. It's 1¼″ thick and has edges that are slightly rounded. You can use this commercially available deck material or standard 2 × 6 lumber. I started with a perimeter of 5/4 decking, and then filled in the hexagon with boards that ran parallel to the entrance. It can be a challenge to cut the six perimeter boards exactly since each end must be notched to fit around one-half of a post. Additionally, the ends of each board are cut at 30° to meet the next piece on either end. The perimeter boards for my gazebo deck were 1¼″ thick by 5½″ wide by 49½″ long, measured between the longest part of the board. I discovered that the simplest method for accurate cutting was to create a cardboard template as illustrated in "Deck Board Layout." Test fit the template on each of the six sides, adjusting if necessary, then cut and attach all six perimeter boards. I installed the perimeter boards leaving them 1½″ over the cedar skirt boards.

Step 8

Deck Board Layout

Step 9

10 Install the remaining deck boards alternately attaching front and back into the middle, leaving a ⅛" gap between the boards. There will be other boards to notch as you reach the posts and all will be angle cut by 30° at each end. You'll often find that the last two boards will not be a full 5½" wide. These boards were each ripped to 3½" wide and attached with ⅛" spacing.

11 Use one of the ripped pieces from the reduced-width center boards as a support under the entrance. This perimeter deck board will experience stress as people walk in and out of the gazebo, so the added support is necessary.

12 Cut ten upper and lower rails at 1½" thick by 3½" wide by 41" long and five cap rails at 1¹₂" thick by 3½" wide by 41¾" long. All rails are cut at 30°. The upper and lower rails are attached with screws, so they are slightly inside the outside face of the post, and the cap rails are flush with the outside face of the posts. See "Rail Positioning."

Step 10

Step 11

Step 12

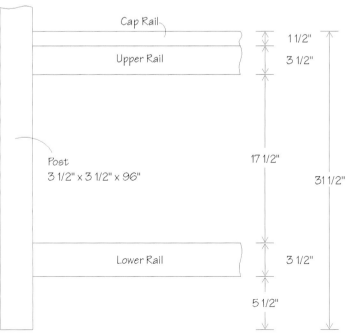

Cap Rail

Upper Rail

1 1/2"

3 1/2"

Post
3 1/2" x 3 1/2" x 96"

17 1/2"

31 1/2"

Lower Rail

3 1/2"

5 1/2"

Rail Positioning

13 Install six wall top plates at 1½″ thick by 3½″ wide by 46″ long at the outside angle. Secure with 3″ coated nails, flush with the outside face of the support boards. Sand the tips of the angle cut, flush with the posts, using a belt sander.

14 Many structures that are hand framed using common rafters have a ridge beam. The rafters meet and are secured to this beam. In the case of a hexagon gazebo, using common rafters that intersect with each other at 60°, a key block is used. A key block is nothing more than a six-sided piece of wood that allows the rafters to meet at the roof's center. The key block is cut from a piece of 4 × 4 on the table saw as shown. Refer to "Key Block Layout" for pattern details. The simplest way to cut the block accurately is to transfer the pattern onto the end of a 4 × 4 and use the lines as a cutting guide to set the saw. The key block is 18″ long and will be trimmed to size after the roof shingles are installed.

Step 13

Step 14

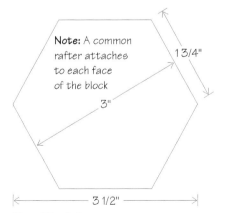

Note: A common rafter attaches to each face of the block

1 3/4″

3″

3 1/2″

Key Block Layout

15 We now need six common rafters that will be cut as described earlier in this chapter. Our common rafter length squared equals the square of the total run plus the square of the total rise. Our total run is 45¼″ and that figure squared equals 2,047.56 inches. The total rise is found by multiplying four times the number of feet in the total run. Since our roof has a 4/12 pitch, we know that it rises 4″ for every foot of total run. The number of feet in the total run equals 45¼″ divided by 12 or 3.77. Therefore, four times 3.77 equals a total rise of 15.08 or 15⅛″. That figure squared equals 227.41. The sum of the squared total run and the total rise equals 2274.97, which is the squared length of the common rafter. By calculating the square root of that number, we know that our common rafter length, which is measured from outside of the wall face to the ridge along the line length as detailed in "Common Rafter Terms" on page 110 is 47¾″. Refer back to "Figuring Rafter Length" on page 111 for calculations. Now, we have two additional issues before we cut the rafter. First, we want to add 12″ behind the bird's mouth plumb cut for our rafter tail overhang. Second, as discussed earlier, we must subtract half the thickness of our key block (ridge beam) at the ridge plumb cut of each common rafter. The rafters will not meet each other directly at the ridge. They all attach to the key block, which we know from "Key Block

Step 15

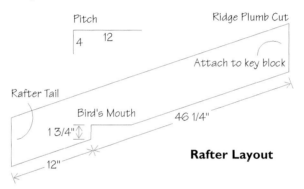

Rafter Layout

Layout" that it separates each opposing rafter by 3″. Therefore, the ridge plumb cut is cut back 1½″ on each rafter to account for the key block thickness. Refer to "Rafter Layout" and cut six common rafters.

16 Attach two opposing rafters to the key block with screws as shown. Mark a line 8″ down from the top of the key block, and attach the rafters with their upper edge even with that line. The key block will be trimmed after the roof shingles are installed.

Step 16

17 Lift the two rafters and key block assembly on the roof, and toe nail the rafters at the bird's mouth into the top plate. Be sure the rafters center on each post. Install the remaining four common rafters, attaching them to the key block and on the post center line.

18 Two hexagon blocks are required, cut from 2 × 8 material. Refer to "Hexagon Block Layout" for pattern details.

19 One hexagon block will be used on the bottom of the key block and one on the top. The top block will be attached after the roof shingles have been applied, so a proper trim height for the key block can be determined. These blocks are decorative although the lower block does provide some structural assistance in tying all of the rafters together. Trim the lower end of the key block so that the hexagon block can be attached. We want the hexagon block to touch each rafter as well as the bottom of the key block. It may take a couple of cuts to achieve a good fit because it's an awkward place to measure. Cut the key block a little longer on the first attempt, judge the fit and then cut small amounts from the key block length until the hexagon block fits properly. You may find that a small sander is useful in reducing the length of the key block as you approach the correct dimension. Attach the hexagon block with seven 3″ exterior screws, one into each rafter and one into the center of the key block.

Step 17

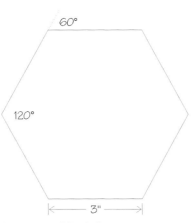

Hexagon Block Layout

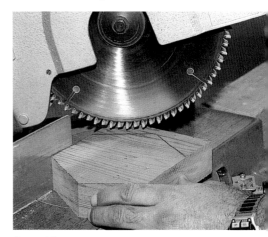

Step 18

Step 19

20 Cut and install six fascia boards. However, use the length dimension as a rough guide only because your distances may be different depending on where the common rafter was attached.

21 The roof sheathing consists of 1 × 4 boards, spaced at 7½″ on center. As detailed earlier, cedar shingles are normally installed on spaced roof sheathing to provide proper air circulation.

22 Attach the boards to the rafters with 2″ galvanized nails. The boards will run between rafters and contact only half the thickness of each rafter, so use two nails at each end of the sheathing board into the rafter. The sheathing boards will have a 30° angle on each end.

23 Start the first row flush with the outside edge of the fascia board. Approximately 42 roof sheathing boards are required, with each row cut progressively shorter as you cover the roof from bottom to top.

Step 20

Step 22

Step 23

24 Begin applying cedar shingles with a 7½" exposure and a double starter course. The starter course extends past the fascia board by 1½". The underside of the sheathing boards are exposed inside the gazebo and roofing nails that are driven through the boards are not visually pleasing, so begin installing the shingles with ¾" galvanized roofing nails. As the thickness of the shingles builds up toward the top of the roof, switch to 1" or 1¼" nails. Refer to the installation procedures in this chapter for installing cedar shingles. If you require more information, contact the Cedar Shake and Shingle Bureau at the address given on page 109.

25 The hip cap shingles are 4" wide and cut from regular shingles. Each shingle is angled on its inside edge at 30°. Start the first course with a double row and overlap the shingles, installing from bottom to top. Use longer roofing nails because of the thickness buildup caused by multiple layers of shingles. Try not to use longer nails than necessary to avoid nailing completely through the roof sheathing.

26 After completing the installation of the hip shingles, trim the key block flush with the last row of shingles. Attach the hexagon block to the key block with two 3" screws. This is mainly a decorative element, but it serves as a rain cap over the key block.

27 The common rafters, sheathing boards and shingles make up the interior "ceiling" of the gazebo. It's important to carefully drive nails and screws so they won't puncture any of the ceiling material.

Step 24

Step 25

Step 27

28 I used 1 × 4 cedar tongue-and-groove boards that had a bead detail to cover five sides of the railing. The boards were cut at 23¾″ long. Use construction adhesive and finishing nails to attach the boards.

29 Cut and install ten boards at ¾″ thick by 3½″ wide by 38½″ long at the bottom and top of the vertical panel boards. Verify the distance on your gazebo before cutting the boards to length. These boards, which are in line with the upper and lower rails, cover the panel board ends and add visual depth to the railing. Once again, use construction adhesive and finishing nails to install these boards.

30 The gazebo is complete. You can let the cedar weather naturally to a gray color or maintain its original look with a clear wood protectant.

Step 28

Step 29

Construction Notes

One issue that must be addressed when building multi-sided structures is that all opposing walls must be as parallel and equal to the others as possible. As illustrated in "Post Layout" on page 114, dimensions A, B and C must be identical. When they are, the hexagon is properly formed with 120° angles at all wall intersections.

Try to keep the six posts plumb as you construct the gazebo. If you're having trouble, temporarily support them with cross bracing. Shim the base level as soon as the rim joists are attached.

Concealing nails and screws can be a challenge when building gazebos, but it's necessary because the structure is the finished product. In house framing, we can hide much of the structural lumber with drywall and floor covering. But as you can see in the photographs, the underside of the rafters, sheathing boards and shingles make up the finished ceiling. Keep that in mind as you build and take a little extra time when fastening joints.

And finally, I know from experience that the mathematics involved in calculating rafter sizes can intimidate some woodworkers. However, review the process as detailed in this chapter until you're comfortable with the concepts. It isn't that difficult. Practice cutting rafters with inexpensive stock until you've mastered the process.

Screened Gazebo

Variations and Options

There are literally hundreds of variations and options involved with the design and construction of gazebos. Hexagon, octagon, square, screened or the addition of fancy scroll trim work are just a few of the many possibilities open to the builder.

For example, in some areas, mosquitoes are a problem and sitting outdoors in the evening isn't very pleasant. However, you can screen the gazebo and use full panels for the railing, which will prevent many of our little flying friends from spoiling a nice evening.

Gazebo designs aren't limited to the hexagon shape. There are many options available, including a square floor plan.

The construction principles apply no matter what design you use at your site, including the common rafter size calculations.

As you can see, gazebos aren't always made from cedar. They can be built with any combination of materials. I've seen some beautiful structures with vinyl siding and even a few metal-clad models.

Design the gazebo to meet your needs since it is a large structure that will be around for a long time. If you plan on doing a lot of entertaining, the size will probably be larger than the project gazebo. But if a quiet spot back in the garden is all you need, then this 8′ plan is ideal.

You aren't necessarily restricted to hand framing a roof, nor do you have to build the gazebo as a stand-alone building. It can be connected to the main deck as shown in the following photograph.

Remember, don't be restricted by what everyone thinks a gazebo should look like—build it to suit your

Square Gazebo

requirements. As you can see in the examples, roof pitch can be at any angle. Railings can be flat, spindle or panel, either down to the floor or slightly raised.

The best design advice is to first determine your family's needs for the structure. Then spend some time looking at different gazebos until you find a combination of features that fill those requirements. Use the best material and hardware your budget will allow, and build your dream gazebo. After all, think about all the years of enjoyment you're going to get from a couple of weeks' work.

Gazebo as Part of a Deck

Index

More Great Books for Your Woodshop!

How to Make $40,000 a Year With Your Woodworking—This guide takes the guesswork out of starting and running your own woodworking enterprise. It provides a solid business program using charts, forms and graphs that illustrate how to define objectives, create a realistic plan, market your work, manage your staff and keep good, accurate records with formulas for projecting overhead, labor costs, profit margins, taxes and more. *#70405/$19.99/30 b&w illus./paperback*

Woodcarving Techniques & Designs—Using just five standard chisels and this guide's clear instructions, traceable templates and full-color photos, you'll be able to produce beautiful woodcarvings. Sixteen different projects teach you a range of techniques for creating relief, incised and three-dimensional carvings. *#70412/$27.99/120 color illus./20 full-size patterns*

How to Design and Build Your Ideal Woodshop—Designed especially for the home-shop woodworker, this guide features dozens of practical alternatives, tips and solutions for transforming attics, garages, basements or out-buildings into efficient and safe woodshops. Clear instructions also include photos, drawings and considerations for electricity, lighting, ventilation, plumbing, accessibility, insulation, flooring and more. *#70397/$24.99/160 pages/paperback*

Building Classic Antique Furniture With Pine—This book offers a range of affordable and user-friendly furniture projects, including antique-style tables, desks, cabinets, boxes, chests and more. Each step-by-step project includes numbered steps with photos and drawings, materials lists, a brief description of the function and history of each piece, and the estimated current market value of both the original piece and the reproduction. *#70396/$22.99/216 color illus./paperback*

The Woodworker's Guide to Shop Math—This hands-on guide takes mathematic principles from the chalkboard to the woodshop, using real-life shop situations to make math easy and practical. Also provided is an overview of basic arithmetic, a review of common units of measurement, and several conversion charts and tables for fractions, multiplication, weights, decimals, volume, area, temperature and more. *#70406/$22.99/169 b&w illus./paperback*

Making Elegant Gifts From Wood—Develop your woodworking skills and make over 30 gift-quality projects at the same time. You'll find everything you're looking to create in your gifts—variety, timeless styles, pleasing proportions and imaginative designs that call for the best woods. Plus, technique sidebars and hardware installation tips make your job even easier. *#70331/$24.99/128 pages/30 color, 120 b&w illus.*

Good Wood Handbook, Second Edition—Now you can select and use the right wood for the job—before you buy. You'll discover valuable information on a wide selection of commercial softwoods and hardwoods—from common uses, color and grain to how the wood glues and takes finish. *#70329/$19.99/128 pages/250 color illus.*

Getting the Very Best From Your Router—Get to know your router inside and out as you discover new jigs and fixtures to amplify its capabilities, as well as techniques to make it the most precise cutting tool in your shop. Plus, tips for comparing different routers and bits will help you buy smart for a solid long-term investment. *#70328/$22.99/144 pages/225+ b&w illus./paperback*

100 Keys to Woodshop Safety—Make your shop safer than ever with this manual designed to help you avoid potential pitfalls. Tips and illustrations demonstrate the basics of safe shopwork—from using electricity safely and avoiding trouble with hand and power tools to ridding your shop of dangerous debris and handling finishing materials. *#70333/$17.99/64 pages/125 color illus.*

Creating Your Own Woodshop—Discover dozens of economical ways to fill unused space with the woodshop of your dreams. You'll learn how to convert space, lay out the ideal woodshop, or improve your existing shop. *#70229/$18.99/128 pages/162 b&w illus./paperback*

Tables You Can Customize—Learn how to build four types of basic tables—from a Shaker coffee table to a Stickley library table—then discover how to apply a wide range of variations to customize the pieces to fit your personal needs. *#70299/$19.99/128 pages/150 b&w illus./paperback*

How to Sharpen Every Blade in Your Woodshop—You know that tools perform best when razor sharp—yet you avoid the dreaded chore. This ingenious guide brings you plans for jigs and devices that make sharpening any blade short and simple! Includes jigs for sharpening boring tools, router bits and more! *#70250/$17.99/144 pages/157 b&w illus./paperback*

The Woodworker's Sourcebook, 2nd Edition—Shop for woodworking supplies from home! This book includes listings for everything from books and videos to plans and associations. Each listing has an address and telephone number and is rated in terms of quality and price. *#70281/$19.99/160 pages/50 illus.*

Basic Woodturning Techniques—Detailed explanations of fundamental techniques like faceplate and spindle turning will have you turning beautiful pieces in no time. *#70211/$14.95/112 pages/119 b&w illus./paperback*

The Stanley Book of Woodworking Tools, Techniques and Projects—Become a better woodworker by mastering the fundamentals of choosing the right wood, cutting tight-fitting joints, properly using a marking gauge and much more. *#70264/$19.95/160 pages/400 color illus./paperback*

Woodworker's Guide to Selecting and Milling Wood—Save money on lumber as you preserve the great tradition of felling, milling and drying your own wood. Loads of full-color illustrations will help you identify the right wood for every job. *#70248/$22.99/144 pages/32 color, 128 b&w illus.*

Good Wood Routers—Get the most from your router with this comprehensive guide to hand-held power routers and table routing. You'll discover a world of information about types of routers, their uses, maintenance, setup, precision table routing and much, much more. *#70319/$19.99/128 pages/550 color illus.*

Tune Up Your Tools—Bring your tools back to perfect working order and experience safe, accurate cutting, drilling and sanding. With this handy reference you'll discover how to tune up popular woodworking machines, instruction for aligning your tools, troubleshooting charts and many other tips. *#70308/$22.99/144 pages/150 b&w illus/paperback*

Other fine Popular Woodworking Books are available from your local bookstore or direct from the publisher. Write to the address below for a FREE catalog of all Popular Woodworking Books. To order books directly from the publisher, include $3.50 postage and handling for one book, $1.50 for each additional book. Ohio residents add 6% sales tax. Allow 30 days for delivery.

Popular Woodworking Books
1507 Dana Avenue
Cincinnati, Ohio 45207

VISA/MasterCard orders call TOLL-FREE
1-800-289-0963

Prices subject to change without notice.   Stock may be limited on some books.

Write to this address for a catalog of Popular Woodworking Books, plus information on *Popular Woodworking* magazine, Woodworker's Book Club, *Writer's Digest* magazine, *Story* magazine, and Writer's Digest School.   3131